LAUGHTER, CON

KLEIST'S *DE*

GM4

Laughter, Comedy and Aesthetics:

Kleist's *Der zerbrochne Krug*

Mark G. Ward

UNIVERSITY OF DURHAM 1989

ISBN 0 907310 22 2

For my parents

Contents

CHAPTER I

THE PROBLEM OF COMEDY

> Le rire ne relève donc pas de l'esthétique pure, puisqu'il poursuit (inconsciemment, et même immoralement dans beaucoup de cas particuliers) un but utile de perfectionnement général. (Henri Bergson)[1]

> Where comedy becomes corrective it is no longer truly comic. (Horace Kallen)[2]

Writing over forty years ago in the *Deutsche Vierteljahrsschrift* in an essay entitled "Die wissenschaftlichen Bemühungen um die Analyse des Komischen", Rommel was prompted in his introductory paragraph to speak of 'der abschreckenden Weitläufigkeit und Unübersichtlichkeit der Literatur über das Komische'; and needless to say the decades since Rommel's work have only served to intensify the problem, with the publication of a further mass of writings on comedy and the comic from the perspectives of a wide variety of disciplines.

Despite, however, the sheer weight of endeavour in the field of

9

analysis of the comic and comedy that he observes up until the time of writing, and with a wry understanding of Jean Paul's observation: 'das Lächerliche habe seit jeher nicht in die Definitionen der Gelehrten eingehen wollen, ausgenommen: unwillkürlich',[3] Rommel is forced to conclude:

> Aber erstaunlicherweise ist diese Diskussion über weite Strecken recht unergiebig . . . Das Miß-trauen der Forscher richtet sich immer nur gegen die Untersuchungen der Vorgänger, die selten ernsthaft geprüft, sondern meist ungeduldig beiseitegeschoben werden. Jeder vertraut nur dem eigenen Einfall; Wiederholungen sind daher häufig, längst erledigte Theorien werden in leichter Abwandlung mit ehrlicher Entdecker-freude von neuem vorgetragen. Dadurch kommt eine gewisse Planlosigkeit und Weitschweifig-keit in die Geschichte dieser Forschung.[4]

And in that respect too, little has changed in the meantime.

Rommel starts his enquiry from the year 1642 and the publication of Hobbes' *De Cive*, disregarding then the fragmentary observations on comedy that have been preserved from antiquity. Yet part of one paragraph in Aristotle's *Poetics* already contains *in nuce* both of the central insights which in one form or another have governed most thinking on the comic down to the present day, as well as the central problems that have dogged, and continue to dog, this area of literary enquiry. For notwithstanding the volume of material produced, the comic mode has long represented something of a Cinderella area in literary studies, certainly not enjoying the highest of reputations and occupying only a very modest position on most scales of aesthetic value.[5] Indeed from the earliest times significant voices have even questioned whether literary comedy should properly be accorded aesthetic status of any kind. Aristotle records the earliest example of this negative evaluation:

Now, then, the successive changes in the history
of tragedy and the men who brought them about
have been recorded; but the analogous
information about the history of comedy is
lacking because the genre was not treated, at the
beginning, as a serious art form.[6]

In the remarks with which Aristotle then follows this observation
there is contained one of the central premises on which the subsequent
relative denigration of the comic mode has been based, that is the
selection of subject matter and the related question of positioning in
terms of sociological categories. In contradistinction to its presumed
antithetical twin, comedy is not seen to draw on public affairs, on high
emotion, on elevated diction, with symbolically representative figures
from the upper strata of society, but rather on a private or domestic
world, on mundane and basic problems, on everyday language, with
recognisable, ordinary types for characters. As a consequence, rather
than articulating a celebration of human uniqueness, of the power of
the human spirit to achieve sublimity and moral freedom, of the
potential of Man to rise above his essentially determined condition,
whether that determination derive from heritage, background, or Man's
position within a metaphysical scheme of Fate and superordinated
forces, comedy is deemed to present images of human frailty, of Man's
baser nature and of his weakness. Rather than concerning itself with
ultimate verities sustained by a commensurately profound ontology,
comedy is seen to have a limited focus dealing with immediate and
pragmatic, and hence ephemeral and philosophically insignificant
issues.

Not only has comedy been deemed inferior in terms of its
material content, its status as the putative antithesis of tragedy has
frequently been described not in a relation of antithetical equivalents,
but in a relation of dependent subordination. Working with a series of
oppositions such as serious/light-hearted, profound/frivolous, eternal/

11

transient, tragedy has been seen as the primary form which establishes the norms on which comedy is reliant. In the words of Kerr: 'Comedy is a parasitical form, and no absolute; it needs a richer form to feed on.'[7] Earlier in his study entitled *Tragedy and Comedy* Kerr formulates the relation between the two forms as follows:

> Comedy wholly loosed from tragedy is, perversely, comedy bastardized. The word is harsh, but because comedy comes into existence as a comment, as a footnote, as a blemish on something greater than itself, it paradoxically loses caste as it turns purer. Comedy and tragedy are not equally independent impulses best developed in contrary directions. The primacy of tragedy permits it to assert itself separately, taking no notice of comedy when it chooses to go unaccompanied. But comedy, being in essence a shadow, requires a body to stand between it and the sun . . .[8]

Moreover in that same section of the *Poetics* Aristotle raises a further matter which has served to pose problems for the classification of comedy as a legitimate form in the aesthetic canon. For Aristotle, as for many in his wake, comedy, at least in a material sense, is seen to hinge on the treatment of 'deformity', 'the ridiculous', 'the ugly and distorted',[9] and so forth, that is, a range of images which are set in differential opposition to the putative concern of 'art', namely 'the beautiful'. This substantive question becomes a particular problem at the time of Romanticism when, in a move away from the eighteenth-century preoccupation with the comic as manifested in short forms such as the anecdote and in the guise of wit, the major thinkers of the time, albeit in their idiosyncratic way, turned their attention to comedy and the comic as a philosophical and existential phenomenon. Notable in this context is the seminal work undertaken by Friedrich Schlegel, in particular his essay of 1794 "Vom ästhetischen Werte der alten griechischen Komödie". On the one hand Schlegel unexceptionally identifies the true function of comedy as being 'eine öffentliche Darstellung des Lächerlichen', with the laughable conceived as something 'Schlechtes und Häßliches', but then he of necessity finds that the comic form is caught up in an insoluble paradox, for it must achieve its aim of creating 'schöne Freude' by negating that on which it relies for its sustaining motive force:

> Es ist die eigentliche Aufgabe der Komödie, das Unvollkommne, welches allein der Freude dramatische Energie verleihen kann, so viel als möglich zu entfernen, zu vergüten oder zu mildern, ohne jedoch die Energie zu vernichten, oder den Mangel der komischen durch tragische Energie zu ersetzen - eine Forderung, die noch nie ganz befriedigt ist.[10]

It is only in a perfect society located in a Utopian future that pure comedy, not dependent on the presentation of imperfection, would be possible, and indeed in such circumstances comedy would represent the highest of all poetic art forms. Unfortunately Schlegel is forced into the admission that such a work in such conditions would no longer represent the comic as he has defined it: '. . . vielmehr an die Stelle des Komischen würde das Entzückende treten . . .'[11]

It is also to this problem that Schiller directs his attention in the treatise dealing specifically with the inclusion of this kind of material in art, "Gedanken über den Gebrauch des Gemeinen und Niedrigen in der Kunst" (1802), where he is led to the conclusion that the nature of the response to this kind of material, 'belustigen', does not fall within what is in his terms an aesthetic response:

> Es gibt zwar Fälle, wo das Niedrige auch in der Kunst gestattet werden kann, da nämlich wo es Lachen erregen soll. Auch ein Mensch von feinen Sitten kann zuweilen, ohne einen verderbten

> Geschmack zu verrathen, an dem rohen aber
> wahren Ausdruck der Natur und an dem Kontrast
> zwischen den Sitten der feinen Welt und des
> Pöbels sich belustigen. Die Betrunkenheit eines
> Menschen von Stande würde, wo sie auch
> vorkäme, Mißfallen erregen; aber ein betrunkener
> Postillion, Matrose und Karrenschieber macht
> uns lachen. Scherze, die uns an einem Menschen
> von Erziehung unerträglich seyn würden,
> belustigen uns im Munde des Pöbels ... Sobald es
> der Dichter bloß auf ein Lachstück angelegt, und
> weiter nichts will, als uns belustigen, so können
> wir ihm auch das Niedrige hingehen laßen, nur
> muß er nie Unwillen oder Eckel erregen.[12]

The aim, then, of comedy as defined here is a lowly one, that of mere entertainment, or in Kantian terms 'Vergnügen', and hence within this idealist tradition of thought on aesthetics *a priori*, whatever the merits of an individual work, unaesthetic.

If the general framework of critical and scholarly commonplace regarding comedy and the comic is not particularly auspicious, the outlook is even bleaker for the specific national tradition of comedy of which *Der zerbrochne Krug* is part. The codes of national stereotyping come to the fore when comedy is discussed in the context of German culture, for the German mentality or temperament is habitually seen to exist as an exclusive opposite of comedy. If George Eliot's observations in her essay, "German Wit: Heinrich Heine", are taken seriously it should be impossible to mention a German comedy and concepts such as structure or the aesthetic in the same breath:

> A German comedy is like a German sentence:
> you see no reason in its structure why it should
> ever come to an end, and you accept the
> conclusion as an arrangement of Providence
> rather than of the author.[13]

What for her German comedy lacks is the vital requisite of form or purposive arrangement, whether that be rhetorical or aesthetic. To such charges may be added the reservations of George Meredith, whose equally low opinion of German comedy draws on the twin sources of aesthetic and moral revulsion:

> German attempts at comedy remind one vividly of Heine's image of his country in the dancing of Atta Troll. Lessing tried his hand at it, with a sobering effect upon readers. The intention to produce the reverse effect is just visible, and therein, like the portly graces of the poor old Pyrenean Bear poising and twirling on his right hind-leg and his left, consists the fun. Jean Paul Richter gives the best edition of the German comic in the contrast of Siebenkäs with his Lenette. A light of the comic is in Goethe; enough to complete the splendid figure of the man, but no more.
> The German literary laugh, like the timid awakenings of their Barbarossa in the hollows of the Untersberg, is infrequent, and rather monstrous - never a laugh of men and women in concert. It comes of the unrefined fancy, grotesque or grim, or gross, like the peculiar humours of their little earthmen. Spiritual laughter they have not yet attained to . . .[14]

While the aspersions of George Eliot and Meredith at least have the saving grace of themselves being suffused with wit and humour, of much greater concern is the failure of the indigenous German critical tradition to establish any coherent defence against this kind of charge. Within the context of the nineteenth-century Hettner, writing in 1852 and drawing substantially on the ideology of nationhood, perceives a decline in comic writing;[15] and just over a decade later in 1863 Hillebrand cites Goethe's dictum: 'Wir können kein Lustspiel haben, weil wir keine Gesellschaft haben' to support his assessment:

> Wenn Italien und Deutschland auf dem Gebiete der Komödiendichtung hinter Dänemark zurückblieben, so ist diese Lücke in der reichen Literatur zweier geistig so fruchtbarer Völker gewiß nur auf das Fehlen der nationalen Einheit und eines Zentrums ihres gesellschaftlichen Lebens zurückzuführen.[16]

The premise of comedy as a social phenomenon and the particularised state of the German area as an obstacle to the development of a successful national comic tradition then leads to the depressing judgement:

> Von Deutschland kann man, ohne fehlzugehen, sagen, daß es nur eine einzige Komödie von hohem Wert hervorgebracht hat: *Minna von Barnhelm*. Weder Goethe noch Schiller, weder Klinger noch Lenz, auch nicht die Romantiker dieses Jahrhunderts und ihre Nachahmer haben eine in der Nation wurzelnde Komödie geschaffen.[17]

In more recent times the influential study of Helmut Arntzen has served to underscore the indigenous denigration of the German comic tradition. The very title of his work conveys both the area and the nature of his concern: *Die ernste Komödie*,[18] for the epithet 'ernst' is here intended to identify a tendency in German comedies which is essentially subversive of their professed identity. Arntzen lists three premises which have governed critical investigation of German comedy from the time of Romanticism onwards. First, it is recognised that German comedies are simply few in number; second, they are qualitatively inferior to tragedies; and the third of the premises runs:

> . . . diese wenigen deutschen Komödien sind bei genauerer Prüfung in Wahrheit Tragödien oder Tragikomödien oder Dramen, die nicht näher zu charakterisieren sind.[19]

The major works which Arntzen cites as falling into this category are *Minna von Barnhelm*, the comedies of Lenz, *Der zerbrochne Krug* and *Amphitryon*, but this process of interpretation against authorial intention can also be extended to *Leonce und Lena, Weh dem, der lügt!* and *Der Schwierige*, and thus the list begins to resemble a complete catalogue of major works of German literature which their respective authors have provided with the generic classification 'Lustspiel'.

In the case of the works listed above the secondary literature abounds with examples of readings which are concerned to undertake what seems to be an act of rescue by attempting to establish analogies between the comedies and the 'serious' writings of their authors.[20] Time and again elements of, say, plot and character which are susceptible to extrapolation and neutral or tragic interpretation are taken and read in isolation, away from the broad sustaining structures of the work as a whole. As a result, these elements are evaluated, not in terms of their structural dependence on the inner form of the works from which they have been divorced, but as autonomous units of meaning. The fragmented nature of this interpretative approach has the further consequence of marginalising any understanding of the comic onto a componential basis. Rather than seeing the comedy of the work as a function of its significant form, as the formulation of an aspect of human experience by the process of symbolisation, comedy is displaced onto peripheral and presumably unintegrated features of the text, such as an aspect of stage business, a joke, or possibly a whole sub-plot. But to all intents and purposes the comedy of the work is not seen as a central constituent of the articulating structure, but as a veneer or gloss, which often overlays what otherwise could be, and what is in reality, according to this mode of reading, essentially a tragic vision.

That a need should be felt to treat such works as *Minna von Barnhelm, Der zerbrochne Krug* and *Weh dem, der lügt!* in this way is but one more expression of a widespread unease with comedy as a literary form. One of the reasons for such unease derives from, or at least receives an early formulation in, as so far all problems have been seen to do, Aristotle's brief comments in the *Poetics*. For Aristotle, as for the vast majority in his wake, the ability to induce laughter, or at least the power to elicit a smile, has been taken as the touchstone for the proof of the comic constitution of a text. Such a premise would on the surface seem to be so obvious a point as not to merit discussion; yet in practice it masks such a variety of divergent strategies and obscures or conflates such a wide range of questions as to render itself at best inadequate, and at worst meaningless. For example, what this tenet is incapable of distinguishing is one of the issues which, albeit very often unspoken, has ebbed and flowed behind discussion of the comic, namely whether the comic is an objective form or whether it only exists in subjective realisations. In other words, and to polarise the issue: is a work comic because we laugh at/with it, or do we laugh at/with it because it is comic?

Perhaps more fundamental is the specific methodological difficulty of taking the physical reaction of laughter as the basis for assertions concerning the psychical disposition which gives rise to it. It could be contended that one of the major sources of confusion in the discussion of comedy arises from an implicit assumption that laughter is always expressive of the same response, and this despite the large number of studies whose aim is to spell out the diversity of causes which prompt this seemingly uniform condition. In the period of positivism Sully's *An Essay on Laughter. Its Forms, Its Causes, Its Development and Its Value*,[21] and Dugas' *Le Rire*,[22] both published in 1902, set out in list form what they perceive as the wide range of types of laughter, and long before them Hegel had observed:

> Überhaupt läßt sich nichts Entgegengesetzteres auffinden als die Dinge, worüber die Menschen lachen. Das Plattste und Abgeschmackteste kann sie dazu bewegen, und oft lachen sie ebensosehr

> über das Wichtigste und Tiefste, wenn sich nur
> irgendeine ganz unbedeutende Seite daran zeigt,
> welche mit ihrer Gewohnheit und täglichen
> Anschauung in Widerspruch steht. Das Lachen ist
> dann nur eine Außerung der wohlfälligen
> Klugheit, ein Zeichen, daß sie auch so weise
> seien, solch einen Kontrast zu erkennen und sich
> darüber zu wissen. Ebenso gibt es ein Gelächter
> des Spottes, des Hohns, der Verzweiflung usf.[23]

More recently McCollom has offered a by no means exhaustive list of
the range of emotion for which laughter is the but external
manifestation:

> Laughter can give rise to happy companionship
> (largely or completely devoid of feelings of
> superiority), friendly greeting, playfulness,
> surprise, shock, tension or fear followed by relief,
> sudden deflation of expectation (or the reverse of
> this - sudden inflation), sudden awareness of
> incongruity, the clash of independent patterns of
> thought (Arthur Koestler's 'bisociation'), release
> of inhibition, Hobbes' 'sudden glory', ironic
> feeling, bitterness, and if Edmund Bergler is
> right, the effective masking from oneself of
> psychic masochism.[24]

Faced with such a myriad of triggers for what is, after all,
intrinsically one of the most absurd of human responses, it is difficult
to discern any point of connection with literary analysis, and perhaps
more importantly, any way in which a pursuit of the causes and nature
physical response can yield any insights or conclusions for literary
scholarship. Indeed Olson is led to discount laughter as a viable
starting point for the investigation of comedy:

> Laughter is not a single emotion; indeed, it is not
> an emotion at all. It is rather, as Spinoza says, a
> physical affection of a certain kind; and it can
> proceed from all sorts of causes, most of which

> do not concern us . . . it is only an unreliable
> external sign of a particular *internal* - I mean
> *psychic* - phenomenon which is our real
> concern.[25]

Despite such reservations about the reliability of laughter as an indicator of the presence of comedy, Olson does at least allow that this physical response, however broad and imprecise it may be as an indicator, is one consideration amongst many others which is appropriate in the context of a discussion of comedy. What is not raised in these qualitative typologies of laughter is the quantitative dimension involving such questions as the relationship of the smile to laughter. For some the relationship of laughter and smiling is only one of degree, so that a work occasioning a smile is no less comic than one causing a resonant belly-laugh. While for others smiling and laughter, albeit bearing close relations to each other, are distinct forms of response and require separate consideration, as do specific forms of the comic such as humour, wit, satire, sarcasm, satire, irony and so forth.[26]

A cautious move away from the assumption of a causal link between laughter and comedy is signalled by Knights in his 'Notes on Comedy', where his concern is not so much with the issue of laughter itself, but rather with the utility of this area of preoccupation as an area of discourse producing a framework of enquiry useful to literary criticism:

> Once an invariable connection between Comedy
> and Laughter is assumed we are not likely to
> make any observation that would be useful as
> criticism. We have only to find the formula that
> will explain laughter, and we know the 'secret' of
> Jonson and Rabelais, Chaucer and Fielding, Jane
> Austen and Joyce.[27]

Within the dialectic of the work-reader relationship in the discussion of comedy, Potts reverses Knights' position of moving from response to texts, the subjective approach, to make much the same point as Knights by doubting the link between the matter of a work and the response of laughter:

> I cannot help thinking that to identify comedy with laughter is to begin at the wrong end . . . the subjects of comedy are not to be identified with the causes of laughter.[28]

Yet despite the methodological reservations of critics such as Knights, Potts and Olson, despite the pragmatic problems of deciding what laughter is and what laughter is expressive of, and despite the repeated suggestion that the causal connection between comedy and laughter should be broken, time and again assertions about or enquiries into the phenomenon of laughter have been used to spawn theories of the comic and comedy, with each in its turn laying claim to exclusive validity. But for all the apparent range and diversity of theory which is then implied by the sheer number of separate studies concerned with this area, there is at root a curious uniformity in the perception of the central structural principle which occasions laughter and which may then be seen as determining comic expression.

At the risk of excessive reductionism it is possible to concur with Sully that all theories of humour and the comic are essentially variants of two main approaches which may be called the moral or degradation theory, and the incongruity theory. The first of these draws its inspiration from the familiar assertion of Hobbes concerning the feeling of 'sudden glory' which arises from the perception of the superiority of the self vis-a-vis the object of the laughter.[29] Whether within the relationship between self and object the emphasis should be placed on the former or latter component will then determine whether this theory is developed into the self-elevation angle of Spencer,[30] or the degradation angle of Bain;[31] but the central premise remains the same, namely that the spectator, whether consciously or unconsciously, whether in an attitude of derision or not, feels himself by virtue of the addition of a perspective not generated from the object itself, that is, in a relationship where dramatic irony is present, to be pre-eminent.

The second theory for which the guiding concept is incongruity is ostensibly more concerned with the operation of ideas than with the moral dimension which feeds into the degradation theory. The trigger mechanism for laughter here is located in the conflict between two habitually incompatible sets or matrices of ideas, which as the result of an event or situation are brought up against each other. The incompatibility creates tension, psychic tension, which can then be released and dispelled in the form of laughter. Yet in practice, as Monro pointed out a quarter of a century ago and Bain many years before him, what passes under the overall heading of incongruity will usually connote the moral dimension of the degradation theory:

> We have suggested that the essence of incongruity is 'universe-changing', the sudden collision of ideas normally kept in different compartments of the mind. And it is true enough that this usually means that some noble, lofty, venerated idea is brought into contact with something trivial or disreputable. Is Bain right, then, in saying that incongruity is really degradation?[32]

And more recently, approaching the question this time from the discipline of psychology, Chapman and Foot have been led to cut through the Gordian knot of proliferating theory by stressing the structural common denominator which ultimately lies behind the myriad of forms of humour and the comic:

> . . . there has been no substantive body of humour which has proved intractable to an incongruity and resolution analysis.[33]

It is possible then to go one stage further than this and to argue that one necessary if not sufficient condition for the generation of laughter is the operation of some form of comparative principle; for if laughter is the physical release of a psychically generated tension, as is generally held to be the case, such tension requires for its initial generation the contrary pull of at least two forces. And that in turn implies the presence of ironic structuration, either in the relationship between spectator and object, or within the object itself which is then subsequently transmitted to the spectator. That ironic foundation can be seen as deriving from the discrepancy between two sets of values, as for example between a form of understanding articulated by a fictional character or situation and the values and understandings which can be taken already to exist in the spectator. It is from this kind of concern that the widespread notion of comedy as a corrective force derives, where actions of a fictional character or characters are shown as aberrant when measured against the norms entertained by the broad social groupings amongst the spectators. Alternatively, the discrepancy may be seen as located initially within different characters set in the fictional work, hence for example the preoccupation within French comic theory with the 'raisonneur' figure, who is seen as supplying the alternative perspective and then communicating this to the audience.

But whatever particular refinements are adduced in the discussion of comic practice, once the allowance is made, on no more persuasive grounds than those of empirical observation, that laughter has to be accommodated within a theory of the comic, although it may only enjoy contingent status, then a central and seemingly insurmountable problem arises for an understanding of comedy as an aesthetic form, where the term 'aesthetic' is understood in terms of its use in the idealist tradition. The stumbling block is summed up, although not fully explicated, by Bullough in his short but seminal essay "'Psychical Distance' as a Factor in Art and an Aesthetic Principle":

> Both to laugh and to weep are direct expressions
> of a thoroughly practical nature, indicating almost
> always a concrete personal affection. Indeed,
> given suitable circumstances and adequate
> distancing-power, both can be distanced, but only
> with great difficulty; nor is it possible to decide
> which of the two offers the greater difficulty. The
> balance seems almost to incline in favour of tears
> as the easier of the two, and this would accord
> with the difficulty of producing a really good
> comedy, or of maintaining a consistent aesthetic
> attitude in the face of a comic situation. Certainly
> the tendency to *under*-distance is more felt in
> comedy even than in tragedy . . .[34]

For Bullough, then, in ways which are not spelled out, it is possible to maintain the requisite psychical distance towards the comic object for the nature of the spectator's relation to that object to be characterised by the necessary disinterest, to be 'cleared of the practical, concrete nature of its appeal', for that relation to be termed aesthetic. The only instance which Bullough cites where works in the comic vein may unquestionably be so constituted as to place the inhibitory aspect between self and object which effects the transformation of material out of the context of personal needs and ends is that of humour. What is curious in his presentation of this point is, however, his recourse to historical development and change as a factor conditioning the nature of the relationship between subject and object:

> In its lower forms comedy is a mere amusement
> and falls as little under the heading of Art as
> pamphleteering would be considered as belles-
> lettres, or a burglary as a dramatic performance.
> It may be spiritualised, polished and refined to
> the sharpness of a dagger-point or the subtlety of
> foil-play, but there still clings to it an atmosphere
> of amusement pure and simple, sometimes of a
> rude, often of a cruel kind. This, together with the

admitted preference of comedy for generalised types rather than individualised figures, suggests the conclusion that its point of view is the survival of an attitude which the higher forms of Art have outgrown. It is noteworthy that this tendency decreases with every step towards high comedy, character-comedy and drama, with the growing spiritualisation of the comic elements and the first appearing of Distance. Historically the development has been slow and halting. There is no doubt that the seventeenth century considered the *Misanthrope* as amusing. We are nowadays less harsh and less socially intolerant and Alceste appears to us no longer as frankly ridiculous. The supreme achievement of comedy is unquestionably that 'distanced ridicule' which we call humour. This self-contradiction of smiling at what we love, displays, in the light vein, that same perfect and subtle balance of the 'antinomy of Distance' which the truly tragic shows in the serious mood.[35]

While it may well be the case that aesthetic form is virtual and not actual, requiring realisation by the percipient in the reciprocal relationship between self and work, and thus changes in what may be deemed to be the practical needs and ends of the percipient from one historical moment to another will affect the attitude that the self holds towards the work, to posit that the attitude of ridicule can as a result undergo the qualitative transformation from interest to disinterest, that is, can be filtered of its practical component, is much more questionable. For while the concept of antinomy of distance expresses the paradox that the relation between self and work is of an unusual kind, 'often highly emotionally coloured, but of a peculiar character', the peculiarity being 'that the personal character has been, so to speak, filtered', having 'been cleared of the practical, concrete nature of its appeal, without, however, thereby losing its original constitution',[36] it is doubtful whether the attitude of ridicule can ever emanate from an exclusion of that concrete, practical orientation. Ridicule involves purposefulness not purposiveness, interest and not disinterest.

This particular problem is addressed by Susanne Langer in her discussion of comedy in *Feeling and Form*, where, drawing on idealist and specifically Schillerian aesthetics, she argues a case for the aesthetic status of comedy against the general tenor of criticism in this area. Having asserted at the outset of her discussion that:

> It is true that tragedy usually - perhaps even always - presents a moral struggle, and that comedy very commonly castigates foibles and vices. But neither a great moral issue, nor folly inviting embarrassment and laughter, in itself furnishes an artistic principle; neither ethics nor common sense produces any image of organic form.[37]

she goes on to an exposition of the problems attending the commonplace assumptions regarding the nature and significance of laughter:

> In comedy the spectator's laugh has only one legitimate source: his appreciation of humour in the piece. He does not laugh with the characters, nor even at them, but at their acts - at their situations, their doings, their expressions, often at their dismay. M. Pagnol holds that we laugh at the characters directly, and regards that as corroboration of his theory: our pleasure in the comic theater lies in watching people to whom we feel superior.
>
> There is, however, one serious defect in that view, namely that it supposes the spectator to be aware of himself as being in the same 'world' as the characters. To compare them, even subconsciously, to himself he must give up his psychical distance and feel himself copresent with them, as one reads an anecdotal news item as something apart from one's own life but still in the actual world, and is moved to say: 'How could she do such a thing! Imagine being so

> foolish!' If he experiences such a reaction in the
> theater, it is something quite aside of his
> perception of the play as a poetic fabrication; he
> has lost, for the moment, his Distance, and feels
> himself inside the picture.
> Humour, then, would be a by-product of comedy,
> not a structural element in it.[38]

But for all the persuasiveness of Professor Langer's arguments on the
nature of the comic rhythm and comic form, which will be discussed
and applied below, her handling of the phenomenon of laughter is
curiously incomplete. She dismisses Pagnol's thesis, and with it that
understanding of long and tenacious lineage which is operating with
some variant of a superiority theory, but is then left with virtually
nothing to put in its place. Laughter, for her, arises from a surge of
vital feeling or is the crest of a wave of felt vitality:

> Laughter, or the tendency to laugh (the reaction
> may stop short of the actual respiratory spasm,
> and affect only the facial muscles, or even meet
> with complete inhibition) seems to arise from a
> surge of vital feeling. This surge may be quite
> small, just so it be enough to be felt distinctly; but
> it may also be great, and not particularly swift,
> and reach a marked climax, at which point we
> laugh or smile with joy. Laughter is not a simple
> overt act, as the single word suggests; it is the
> spectacular end of a complex process. As speech
> is the culmination of a mental activity, laughter is
> a culmination of feeling - the crest of a wave of
> felt vitality.[39]

Such an explanation is, however, remarkably undialectical, for
nowhere can it accommodate the truism that laughter is the physical
release of a psychically engendered tension. In its formulation her
thesis is almost an echo of the arguments of Kallen who, on the
premise of a similarity between the facial expressions involved in
laughter or the smile and the attitude of a triumphant beast about to

devour its prey, hypothesises: 'Laughter is perhaps a mutation from feeding, and it serves the same result; it strengthens life by heightening its vitality'.[40] Kallen is then led, however, to observe that such an enhancement of vitality results from rendering ineffectual that which had seemed dangerous, a process which subsumes an assertion of superiority through degradation. Without such a rider laughter as a tension-release mechanism remains without a cause, yet in its dependence on the circumstances of triumph and defeat it inevitably returns to the assumption of a comparative exercise and the assertion of superiority as the result of such a comparison. The distinction made by Kallen, namely that the comic laughter-giving force lies not in the process of correction, the form which triumph takes when realised in a social context such as that of the fiction of comedy, but rather in the simple joy of the corrector or victor, by which tenet laughter is to be divested of the imputation of mockery, malice or degradation, is little more than an exercise in sophistry. The joy must derive from the situation of a danger overcome, a readily identifiable and concrete source, and is thus not a purely subjective condition engendered from within the individual; laughter derives from the reciprocity of self and situation.

Faced with this apparently insoluble dilemma in which it is recognised that irony is a necessary condition of comedy, and yet that the operation of irony as conventionally understood involves a relation between percipient and work which because of its nature as an exercise of interested comparison precludes the presence of psychical distance and hence of an aesthetic attitude, the simplest expedient would be to have recourse to the authority of a figure such as Theodor Lipps in whom the reservations about any form of connection between comedy and laughter might be said to have culminated. In his substantial treatise *Komik und Humor. Eine psychologisch-ästhetische Untersuchung* published in 1898 and subsequently to influence Freud in his analysis of jokes and wit, Lipps concludes with the unequivocal statement: 'Das Lachen als solches . . . ist für das Verständnis des Komischen völlig bedeutungslos'.[41] With a little more caution Potts expressed a similar sentiment in 1949 when he stated that it was 'very doubtful whether the end of comedy is to produce laughter'.[42] For all the usefulness of such questioning in provoking discussion on the nature of the link between comedy and laughter, some account must be taken of the bald empirical fact that works designated by their authors as 'Komödien', 'Lustspiele', etc, do prompt laughter more frequently than works grouped together under other generic headings.

The conclusion then suggests itself that, given the wide range of objections that may be brought to bear on the thesis that a work of comedy may legitimately lay claim to the status of an aesthetic object, the overwhelming body of opinion and argument must lead to a rejection of that thesis. Yet no less an aesthetician than Schiller, and notwithstanding his statements quoted above from "Gedanken über den Gebrauch des Gemeinen und Niedrigen in der Kunst", claims in *Uber naive und sentimentalische Dichtung* in contrast to the traditional rank-order proposed in the age-old dispute about the relative merits of comedy and tragedy, that it is the former that aspires to the highest goal:

> Wenn also die Tragödie von einem wichtigern Punkt ausgeht, so muß man auf der andern Seite gestehen, daß die Comödie einem wichtigern Ziel entgegen geht, und sie würde, wenn sie es erreichte, alle Tragödie überflüßig und unmöglich machen.[43]

More specifically, comedy and the associated response of laughter are for Schiller far from being seen as the result of restrictive personal affection, rather they are in the last analysis an expression of that freedom of spirit or 'Gemütsfreiheit' which lies at the heart of Schiller's aesthetic theory:

> Ihr Ziel ist einerley mit dem Höchsten, wornach
> der Mensch zu ringen hat, frey von Leidenschaft
> zu sein, immer klar, immer ruhig um sich und in
> sich zu schauen, überall mehr Zufall als Schicksal
> zu finden, und mehr über Ungereimtheit zu
> lachen als über Boßheit zu zürnen oder zu
> weinen.[44]

NOTES

1. H. Bergson, *Le Rire. Essai sur la signification du comique*, (Paris, 1969), pp. 15f.
2. H. Kallen, "The Aesthetic Principle in Comedy", *The American Journal of Psychology*, 22 (1911), 149.
3. J. Paul, *Vorschule der Ästhetik* in J. P., *Werke*, edited by N. Miller, (München, 1960ff), V, 102.
4. O. Rommel, "Die wissenschaftlichen Bemühungen um die Analyse des Komischen", *DVjs*, 21 (1943), 162.
5. See P. Hofmann, "Das Komische und seine Stellung unter den ästhetischen Gegenständen', *Zeitschrift für Ästhetik und allgemeine Kunstwissenschaft*, 9 (1914), 457.
6. Aristotle, *Poetics*, translated by L. Golden, (Eaglewood Cliffs, 1968), p. 10.
7. W. Kerr, *Tragedy and Comedy*, (New York, 1967), pp. 314-5.
8. Ibid., p. 212.
9. Aristotle, p. 9.
10. F. Schlegel, "Vom ästhetischen Wert der griechischen Komödie' in *Kritische-Friedrich-Schlegel-Ausgabe*, edited by E. Behler, (Paderborn, 1979), Erste Abteilung, I, 27.
11. Ibid., 30.
12. F. Schiller, "Gedanken über den Gebrauch des Gemeinen und Niedrigen in der Kunst" in *Schillers Sämtliche Schriften*, edited by K. Goedeke, (Stuttgart, 1867ff.), X, 209f.
13. G. Eliot, "German Wit: Heinrich Heine" in *The Works of George Eliot*, edited by J. W. Cross, (London, n.d.), XII, 73.
14. G. Meredith, *An Essay on Comedy and the Uses of the Comic Spirit*, (London, 1897), p. 57.
15. H. Hettner, *Das moderne Drama*, (Braunschweig, 1852).
16. K. Hillebrand, "Die klassische Komödie und ihre Voraussetzungen" in *Komödie und Gesellschaft*, edited by N. Altenhofer, (Frankfurt am Main, 1973), p. 76.

17. Ibid.
18. H. Arntzen, *Die ernste Komödie. Das deutsche Lustspiel von Lessing bis Kleist*, (München, 1968).
19. Ibid., p. 9.
20. See, for example, O. Mann, "Lessing: Minna von Barnhelm" in *Das deutsche Drama*, I, edited by B. v. Wiese, (Düsseldorf, 1958), pp.79 - 100, and G. Fricke, "Lessings 'Minna von Barnhelm'" in G.F., *Studien und Interpretationen*, (Frankfurt am Main, 1956), pp. 25 - 46.
21. J. Sully, *An Essay on Laughter. Its Forms, Its Causes, Its Development and Its Value*, (London, 1902).
22. L. Dugas, *Le Rire*, (Paris, 1902).
23. G. W. F. Hegel, *Ästhetik II*, (Frankfurt am Main, n.d.), p. 552.
24. W. G. McCollom, *The Divine Average. A View of Comedy*, (Cleveland/London, 1971), p. 32.
25. E. Olson, *The Theory of Comedy*, (Bloomington/London, 1968), p.10.
26. L. C. Knights, "Notes on Comedy" in *Determinations*, edited by F. R. Leavis, (London, 1934), p. 10.
27. See R. Boston, *An Anatomy of Laughter*, (London, 1974), p. 16: 'Laughter is not the same thing as smiling, or humour, or wit, or comedy, though it has obvious close relations with all of them.'
28. L. J. Potts, *Comedy*, (London, 1948), p. 19.
29. T. Hobbes, *Leviathan*, (Harmondsworth, 1968), p. 125.
30. H. Spencer, "Physiology of Laughter", *Macmillan's Magazine*, 1860, I, 395.
31. A. Bain, *Emotions and the Will*, (London, 1859).
32. D. H. Munro, *Argument of Laughter*, (Melbourne, 1959), p. 91.
33. *Humour and Laughter: Theory, Research and Applications*, edited by A. J. Chapman and H. C. Foot, (London, 1976), p. 14.
34. E. Bullough, "'Psychical Distance' as a Factor in Art and an Aesthetic Principle" in E. B., *Aesthetics*, edited by E. M. Wilkinson, (London, 1957), pp. 121-2.
35. Ibid., p. 122.
36. Ibid., p. 97.
37. S. Langer, *Feeling and Form*, (London, 1953), p. 326.
38. Ibid., p. 341.
39. Ibid., p. 340.
40. Kallen, op. cit., pp. 156-7.
41. Th. Lipps, *Komik und Humor. Eine psychologisch-ästhetische Untersuchung*, (Hamburg/Leipzig, 1898), p. 64.

42.   Potts, op. cit., p. 19. See also M. C. Swabey, *Comic Laughter. A Philosophical Essay*, (New Haven/London, 1961), p. 26: 'the mere power to elicit jollity accompanied by a respiratory spasm is hardly sufficient to distinguish the comic.'
43.   Schiller, op. cit., X, 462.
44.   Ibid.

CHAPTER II

A MODEL OF COMEDY

Perhaps because of the concentration on laughter, perhaps because of
the concern with the social function of comedy, perhaps because of the
preoccupation with the rhetorical forms which underlie comic
expression, and certainly because of the persistent suspicion with
which comedy has been viewed throughout the ages, the question of
what might constitute the organic of aesthetic form of comedy has
received relatively little attention. In the wake of the eighteenth-
century empirical tradition comic theory has shown itself much happier
in dealing with short forms - the joke, the anecdote, an individual scene
or situation - but rarely have critics pursued the possibility that a comic
work may as a structured integrated whole be a symbolic expression of
living form, an aesthetic realisation of significant form. That, within
one tradition of understanding, comedy may aspire to such status, is
attested by Schiller's observations quoted at the end of the previous
chapter, and, more fundamentally, is enshrined in a central tenet of his
aesthetic theory. In the XXII Aesthetic Letter Schiller writes:

> Darinn eben zeigt sich der vollkommene Styl in
> jeglicher Kunst, daß er die specifischen
> Schranken derselben zu entfernen weiß, ohne
> doch ihre specifischen Vorzüge mit aufzuheben,

> und durch eine weise Benutzung ihrer Eigen-
> thümlichkeit ihr einen mehr allgemeinen
> Charakter ertheilt.[1]

If this assertion concerning the potential for the various art forms in their highest manifestations simultaneously to retain and yet to transcend their specific characteristics as determined by their respective media is valid, then such potential must be equally present in the various genres within the same basic form which uses the same medium. On such a premise there is no reason why, for example, dramatic comedy should be less aesthetic in constitution and effect than, say, a lyric poem, a novel or a tragedy. It is then perhaps not surprising that the most persuasive of modern critics to have argued the case for comedy, Susanne Langer in her study *Feeling and Form*, should stand in a direct line of descent from Schiller.[2]

She does not, however, stand alone; for additional valuable insights are provided by Northrop Frye in the *Anatomy of Criticism*,[3] Ludwig Jekels in an essay entitled "On the Psychology of Comedy",[4] and Martin Grotjahn in *Beyond Laughter. Humor and the Sub-conscious*.[5] One interesting point regarding these four studies is that they were all originally published in the 1950s, reflecting firstly in their manner of approach and their preoccupation with deep structures the general tendency of thought at the time as witnessed for example in the work of linguisticians and in the slowly emerging method of structuralism, and secondly articulating in their ideological focus a tenor of thought which may be presumed to have derived from the assimilation and working out of the events of the 1930s and 1940s, since, although the word is not a particularly happy choice, each identifies one of the major thrusts of comedy as being its anti-authoritarian ideology. Despite, then, the aim of normative analysis and definition of the comic form, each of these theories can be seen as betraying historically conditioned origins.

In the introduction to a recent collection of analyses of major examples of German comedy Walter Hinck argues precisely this point, namely that theories of comedy, presumably in his terms no less than the works themselves, are inextricably bound up with the intellectual traditions from which they derive, and hence can lay claim to no more than historical and relative validity rather than enjoying normative status:

> Alle Definitionsversuche zum Komischen und zu Komödie bieten, unter verschiedener philosophisch-theoretischer Perspektive, nur Teilansichten. Und alle Definitionen sind letztlich nur schlüssig in dem System des Denkens, aus dem sie hervorgehen. Die Summe der so gewonnenen Ansichten ergibt noch nicht das Ganze. Die Historizität von Komik und Komödie und die Begrenztheit, das geschichtlich Vermittelte unserer Erkenntnis verbieten überhaupt dogmatische Festschreibungen. Gerade der Zukunftsaspekt, der Entwurf-Charakter der Komödie verlangt es, die Vorstellungen von dem, was sie sein soll, offen zu halten.[6]

Yet it is surely ironic that Hinck should argue for a relative historical approach by appealing to a recurrent and arguably normative feature of the genre, its 'Zukunftsaspekt', and moreover a feature which is seen as central in the work of both Frye and Susanne Langer. For it is the provisional or future-oriented character of the comic structure which is seen in their analyses as a primary distinction from the tragic rhythm which is closed and final. For them, however, this radically different 'Gestalt' of time is but one necessary aspect of the genre which is consequent on the different image of organic form which is expressed in, or symbolised by, the comic mode. For whereas tragedy bespeaks a vision in which the nodal centre is constituted by a concern with an individual fate under the perspective of a unique death-bound career, that is, as a fate shaped essentially in advance, the comic vision draws its sustenance from a pattern which is more episodic, circular rather than linear, and in which what is presented is an image of living vitality or 'élan vital', which in its self-assertion restores lost equilibrium and implies a new future. As an image of continuity re-presenting the organic form or basic biological pattern of teleological purpose directed towards self-preservation and self-restoration, the comic form can be seen not only as the antithesis but also as the mirror of tragedy. This relation is, moreover, not restricted to the underlying structure of feeling thus articulated, it also informs the details of the construction of that image in the individual works.

The assertion of continuity and the creation of an image of livingness requires what amounts to a reversal of the structures which determine the archetypal tragic situation as crystallised in the Oedipus story. Both Jekels and Grotjahn cite the significant role played by Freud in isolating the psychological analogues which inhere in the tragic form, and they see the principle of inversion at work in the structures sustaining comic expression. What may possibly be the most important aspect of this inversion concerns a reorientation of the balance of power associated with the generation axis in tragedy and the values associated with that axis:

> . . . the feeling of guilt which, in tragedy, rests
> upon the son, appears in comedy displaced on the
> father; it is the father who is guilty.[7]

Jekels goes on to observe that the signifier connoting moral guilt often assumes the form of a monetary debt, a connotation all the more obvious in the context of German with the dual meaning of the word 'Schuld' as both guilt and debt. To take but three examples of major German comedies: this motif is extensively worked in Lessing's *Minna von Barnhelm* where Tellheim's financial straits and the consequences for his relationship with Minna arise from the King's false assumption as to his character and the resultant financial penalty, in addition to which the motif of the father/son relationship is here invoked in extended form. Equally this monetary dimension figures in Grillparzer's *Weh dem, der lügt!* in the guise of the sum which Gregor is required to pay but fails to raise for the release of Atalus, who is repeatedly characterised as effectively a son to Gregor, whom in turn Grillparzer originally projected as Atalus' father.[8] And finally the motif of monetary debt occurs in *Der zerbrochne Krug* in the way in which Adam, presumably in connivance with Licht, has been abusing his position of authority by carrying out illegal collections.

This transference in the comic mode of guilt onto the father figure, or at one remove a figure or principle of authority, is often mediated through perhaps the most common body of material to be found in the primary dramatic action of comic drama, the love relationship centred on the axis of youth, which after initial frustration and complication eventually comes to fruition. Thus within comic structuration the basic narrative typology or plot sequence of equilibrium, disruption and restoration of equilibrium is given its specific significance through its articulation to a nexus of relations signalling the triumph of vitality over petrification, the triumph of youth over age, the triumph of flexibility and dynamic accommodation over fixity and rigidity. Moreover, the structuring of the dramatic action within comedy with the tendency towards unincremental repetition, or an additive episodic structure, can be seen as the opposite of the essentially linear pattern of the tragic form, in which capacity it sustains the themes of continuity and triumphant vitality by creating an image in which youth assumes a new kind of dominance, marked by an open-ended closure and celebrated in some kind of festival or ritual. It is completely consonant with the value system of comedy that such a festival or ritual should often assume the form of marriage, or at least the striking of an alliance, thus confirming the dominance of vitality and articulating, in the orientation on the future, an awareness of continuity.[9]

What is crucial in the analyses of the critics whose work is summarised above is the recognition of comedy not as a succession of situations based on the unitary configuration of the joke and hence susceptible to the same kind of psychological analysis as is brought to bear on that form of humour, but as a deep symbolic structure which voices fundamental aspects of human experience and has a significant form which is both conditioned by and which conditions the aspect which the constituent elements of the work assume. Thus, simply to identify elements of plot in isolation will not produce adequate distinctions for determining the comic constitution of a work since, as is widely recognised, familiar topoi of the dramatist's craft such as misunderstanding, confusion and ignorance are as at home in tragedy as they are in comedy. The traditional counter to this phenomenon, namely that any pain or injury which results in the course of the dramatic action should not be permanent or too severe, goes only part of the way towards explaining how these situations are handled in comedy. Of much greater moment is the realisation that such situations, which in comedy both can be and indeed are required to be seen as containing at least the potential for tragic development, cannot be divorced from the meaning-generating structure which is the whole work, in which context they assume meanings at variance with their unfulfilled or undeveloped tragic potential, despite perhaps broad affinities with ostensibly similar situations in other works where the issue is a tragic resolution.

But for all the persuasiveness of such understandings of what might constitute the organic aesthetic form of comedy, and for all the necessary correctives they contain to the still dominant view of comedy as an inferior and ultimately sub-literary form, they do not, as argued above, provide of themselves any thoroughgoing rationale as to why the response of laughter should predominate in this genre, nor do they cope with the central problem posed by laughter, namely that, when conventionally seen as an expression of direct affection, it can only indicate an absence of psychical distance and the presence of an interested practical concern. What they could be said to provide in interpreting comedy as an image of livingness and vitality, is a necessary condition but not a sufficient cause for the generation of laughter. If laughter is to be accommodated within an understanding of comedy as an aesthetic form, then it would appear that the trigger mechanism has to be sought not in the final effect of any one individual work, in the perception of its organic form, but rather in the means by which in a reciprocal relation between percipient and text that effect is achieved, which approach then necessitates consideration of the rhetorical strategy which the author employs. That is to say, laughter is not the end product of comedy in the simple sense that an audience laughs at the conclusion of a work, rather laughter is an expression of a psychical state which precedes the conclusion and the perception of organic form.

Starting from a consideration of the qualitative difference in the subject matter appropriate to a comedy and to a tragedy, the former being of no account when compared to the latter, Schiller asserts that it is the task of the comic poet to ensure from the very outset that he treat his material in an aesthetic way, and that as a result the receiving audience, unlike that of a tragedy, never be exposed to direct affection:

> Es ist mehrmals darüber gestritten worden, welche von beyden, die Tragödie oder die Comödie, vor der andern den Rang verdiene. Wird damit bloß gefragt, welche von beyden das wichtigere Objekt behandle, so ist kein Zweifel, daß die erstere den Vorzug behauptet; will man aber wissen, welche von beyden das wichtigere Subjekt erfodre, so muß der Ausspruch eben so entscheidend für die letztere ausfallen. - In der Tragödie geschieht schon durch den Gegenstand sehr viel, in der Comödie geschieht durch den

Gegenstand nichts und alles durch den Dichter. Da nun bey Urtheilen des Geschmacks der Stoff nie in Betrachtung kommt, so muß natürlicher weise der ästhetische Werth dieser beyden Kunstgattungen in umgekehrtem Verhältniß zu ihrer materiellen Wichtigkeit stehen. Den tragischen Dichter trägt sein Objekt, der komische hingegen muß durch sein Subjekt das seinige in der ästhetischen Höhe erhalten. Jener darf einen Schwung nehmen, wozu so viel eben nicht gehöret; der andre muß sich gleich bleiben, er muß also schon dort seyn, und dort zu Hause seyn, wohin der andre nicht ohne einen Anlauf gelangt . . . Diese Freyheit des Gemüths in uns hervorzubringen und zu nähren, ist die schöne Aufgabe der Comödie, so wie die Tragödie bestimmt ist, die Gemüthsfreyheit, wenn sie durch einen Affekt gewaltsam aufgehoben worden, auf ästhetischem Wege wieder herstellen zu helfen. In der Tragödie muß daher die Gemüthsfreyheit künstlicherweise und als Experiment künstlich aufgehoben werden, weil sie in der Herstellung derselben ihre poetische Kraft beweißt; in der Comödie hingegen muß verhütet werden, daß es niemals zu der Aufhebung der Gemüthsfreyheit komme.[10]

Thus, he concludes, the greater must be the art of the comic poet who treats material which inclines towards the pathetic or direct affection, a conclusion which bears on the conventional wisdom that what has been termed comedy of character is the highest and also the most difficult manifestation of the comic genre, since in that particular form the poet does not have the inbuilt inhibitory advantage of dealing with types, but is treating individually realised characters.

While allowing for its presentation in little more than a series of asides and moreover in a work, *Über naive und sentimentalische Dichtung*, which Schiller regarded essentially as one of popularisation, this model of the way in which comedy operates is peculiarly undialectical, and in that bias it can be seen as reflecting the same weakness that has bedevilled comic theory down the years, namely the tendency towards polarisation between subject and object, the view that comedy is either exclusively embedded in the work, or alternatively is exclusively created by the subject. At one extreme are those theories, of which Bergson and Meredith are perhaps the best known examples, which concentrate on the social content of comedy, seeing in it a corrective force, and which locate the comic within the material itself. The opposite pole to such object orientation is represented by those theories which trace the comic response to something which is exclusively engendered from within the receiving subject, whether it be the 'sudden glory' of Hobbes, the physical sense of well-being described by Kant, or a pre-conscious link with the infantile as in Freud. Yet, despite this reservation, Schiller's aesthetic theories do nevertheless yield criteria for a more dialectical understanding of the nature and operation of comedy.

The present context is not the forum for an exposition of Schiller's many writings on matters aesthetic, but as has been frequently pointed out, his thought circles time and again around a limited number of central concepts. In the *Aesthetic Letters* his enquiry is driven by the pressing knowledge and experience of Man's fragmented state and, in the words of Wilkinson and Willoughby: 'What Schiller is demanding is the restoration of the wholeness and harmony characteristic of the individual Greek', a state in which the fragmentation and specialisation of the psyche, necessary concomitants of the modern world, could momentarily be held in abeyance as in the aesthetic mode Man enjoys pure determinability. The antecedents to Schiller's vision are many and varied, and not the least amongst them is the figure of Kant, for whom the aesthetic condition was distinguished by the free play of all the faculties. But Schiller does move significantly away from Kant in countering the latter's tendency towards arid formalism, and does so by employing one very telling image to express that inner state of harmonious equilibrium between affection and reflection, or 'Stofftrieb' and 'Formtrieb'. The definition of the aesthetic occurs in the twentieth letter:

> Das Gemüth geht also von der Empfindung zum Gedanken durch eine mittlere Stimmung über, in welcher Sinnlichkeit und Vernunft zugleich thätig sind, eben deswegen aber ihre bestimmende Gewalt gegenseitig aufheben und durch eine Entgegensetzung eine Negation bewirken. Diese mittlere Stimmung, in welcher das Gemüth weder physisch noch moralisch genöthigt und doch auf beyde Art thätig ist, verdient vorzugsweise eine freye Stimmung zu heißen; und wenn man den Zustand sinnlicher Bestimmung den physischen, den Zustand vernünftiger Bestimmung aber den logischen und moralischen nennt, so muß man diesen Zustand der realen und aktiven Bestimmbarkeit den ästhetischen heißen.[11]

Such a state of determinability can be achieved in one of two ways, either by negating all content, or alternatively by balancing it:

> Er muß also, um Leiden mit Selbstthätigkeit, um eine passive Bestimmung mit einer aktiven zu vertauschen, augenblicklich von aller Bestimmung frei sein, und einen Zustand der bloßen Bestimmbarkeit durchlaufen, weil man, um von Minus zu Plus fortzuschreiten, durch Null den Weg nehmen muß. Mithin muß er auf gewisse Weise zu jenem negativen Zustand der bloßen Bestimmungslosigkeit zurückkehren, in welchem er sich befand, ehe noch irgend etwas auf seinen Sinn einen Eindruck machte. Jener Zustand aber war an Innhalt völlig leer, und jetzt kommt es darauf an, eine gleiche Bestimmungslosigkeit, und eine gleich unbegrenzte Bestimmbarkeit mit dem größtmöglichen Gehalt zu vereinbaren, weil unmittelbar aus diesem Zustand etwas positives erfolgen soll. Die Bestimmung, die er durch Sensation empfangen, muß also festgehalten werden, weil er die Realität nicht verlieren darf, zugleich aber muß sie, insofern sie Begrenzung

> ist, aufgehoben werden, weil eine unbegrenzte
> Bestimmbarkeit statt finden soll. Die Aufgabe ist
> also, die Determination des Zustandes zugleich
> zu vernichten und beyzubehalten, welches nur auf
> die einzige Art möglich ist, daß man ihr eine
> andere entgegensetzt. Die Schalen einer Wage
> stehen gleich, wenn sie leer sind; sie stehen aber
> auch gleich, wenn sie gleiche Gewichte
> enthalten.[12]

A similar image of balance is employed in the short essay "Über den Gebrauch des Chors in der Tragödie", with the significant modification that it here assumes something of a more dynamic character. Having posited that 'das Poetische . . . liegt gerade in dem Indifferenzpunkt des Ideellen und Sinnlichen', Schiller goes on to observe:

> . . . denn wenn die zwey Elemente der Poesie das
> Ideale und Sinnliche nicht innig verbunden
> zusammen wirken, so müssen sie neben einander
> wirken, oder die Poesie ist aufgehoben. Wenn die
> Waage nicht vollkommen inne steht, da kann das
> Gleichgewicht nur durch eine Schwankung der
> beiden Schaalen hergestellt werden.[13]

Both modes of combination, 'zusammen' and 'nebeneinander' imply simultaneity, static balance, and that implication is borne out by the subsequent explanation of the essay:

> Denn das Gemüth des Zuschauers soll auch in der
> heftigsten Passion seine Freiheit behalten, es soll
> kein Raub der Eindrücke seyn, sondern sich
> immer klar und heiter von Rührungen scheiden,
> die es erleidet.[14]

and:

> Dadurch, daß der Chor die Theile aus einander
> hält, und zwischen die Passionen mit seiner
> beruhigenden Betrachtung tritt, gibt er uns unsre
> Freiheit zurück, die im Sturme der Affekte
> verloren gehen würde.[15]

Yet the concept of fluctuation, 'Schwankung', implies of necessity not simultaneity and stasis, but rather a dynamic relation of inequivalence between forces or drives, which then in linear time settle to balance or 'Heiterkeit'.

If the image of the scales and the aspect of dynamic balancing is transposed by analogy to the image of the line of aesthetic distance, then that dynamic balancing can be seen as corresponding in terms of both the constitution and perception of a work to variability along that line. That variability relates to movement between the mode in which which the individual is passively receptive, practically interested and an integral part of the world of sense, and the aesthetic mode in which distance is created by virtue of the operation of reflection, and in which the immediacy of affection yields to a perception of form, of permanence and significance on the basis of and through the world of sense, in Schiller's words 'lebende Gestalt', or in Susanne Langer's terms 'felt thought':

> Die Nothwendigkeit der Natur, die ihn [Man] im
> Zustand der bloßen Empfindung mit ungetheilter
> Gewalt beherrschte, läßt bei der Reflexion von
> ihm ab, in den Sinnen erfolgt ein augenblicklicher
> Friede, die Zeit selbst, das ewig Wandelnde, steht
> still, indem des Bewußtseyns zerstreute Strahlen
> sich sammeln, und ein Nachbild des Unendlichen,
> die Form, reflektiert sich auf dem vergänglichen
> Grunde.[16]

That simple pattern of emergence from passive affection to a perception of form outlined in the above quotation approximates to the sequence which Schiller attributes to the genre of tragedy in the extract already cited from *Über naive und sentimentalische Dichtung*. Once, however, the principle of variability or fluctuation is allowed, as the image of the scales and the associated 'Schwankung' implies it must be, that is, once it is conceded that a consistently aesthetic attitude throughout the duration of a work is not necessary, although, of course, the aesthetic condition remains the goal, the question arises as to whether such fluctuation or variability has to be limited to one single qualitative change from affection to freedom and the perception of form, or whether it is not possible to conceive of this fluctuation in terms of repeated oscillation, or repeated movement back and fore along the line of aesthetic distance.

If the possibility of such repeated oscillation is a tenable proposition, then what is of importance in terms of comic theory and the associated question of the significance of laughter, is that the conditions are given for the creation of an ironic relation in the percipient of the work. For as was observed above, it is common ground across a whole range of theories of comedy that irony is the fundamental prerequisite for the generation of psychical tension and hence laughter. But equally important for the understanding of comedy as an aesthetic form is that this ironic relation is of a very special kind. The irony resulting from this qualitative change in the mode of interaction between percipient and work from passive affection to distanced reflection would neither focus on, nor derive from, aspects of the work such as characters, situations and events in isolation. When an ironic relation of that kind is applied in the theory of comedy it quickly becomes subsumed under the heading of dramatic irony, which, as is argued in Susanne Langer's refutation of Pagnol's theory, requires the co-presence of percipient and work, whence it is only a short step to the structural tenet of comparison and thence to the superiority and corrective theories. Rather the ironic relation as conceived here, with the associated awareness of incongruity, focusses on the substance of the work as a whole, and is realised in the form of vacillation between an interested and an involved response on the one hand, and on the other a qualitatively different relation to the same material, in which such a response is balanced or counteracted by a disinterested and distanced reflective response achieved by the interposing of psychical distance. Such vacillation between two modes of relation to the same material, which eventually settles in favour of 'Gemütsfreiheit' through the perception of 'Schein' and significant form, then functions as the mechanism for the creation of tension, that is a tension centred on the manner of composition and perception of the work as a structured whole and not on isolated aspects of it; incongruity is realised in the perceiving subject in the fluctuation between an involved and a disinterested relation to the work.

Within that shifting relation there are then times at which psychical energy is created because of the mobilisation of practical interests, that is, times when the affect of the material, the engagement of the 'Stofftrieb', predominates. But equally there are times at which, because of the qualitative change of relation to the perception of form, such psychical energy becomes superfluous and available for discharge. The specific form of that discharge, in comedy the form being laughter, is then not antithetical to, but is rather a function of the perception of aesthetic or organic form, the symbolic image of livingness, vitality and harmonious balance. Under such a heading laughter then becomes not a sign of direct affection, but on the contrary a signal of the release of the subject from that affection.

It is one of the commonplaces of literature on this subject that laughter does represent some kind of release, although rarely is this specified beyond generalities. Lipps, and in his wake Freud, trace this pattern to the discharge of excess psychical energy:

> Das Übergewicht der Verfügbarkeit der psych-
> ischen Kraft über die Inanspruchnahme derselben
> ist Grund der Lust und läßt zugleich dies Gefühl
> den Charakter des Heiteren, Leichten, Spielenden

gewinnen.[17]

This particular statement is important for the distinction it makes between the psychological process responsible for the generation of laughter and the nature of the condition finally achieved by the subject, and thus it signals the necessity of not conflating process and end. However, Lipps' argument concerning the process by which the psychical energy is rendered superfluous differs fundamentally from that which has been argued above concerning a qualitative change in the relation between subject and object as direct affection yields to freedom, as practical orientation is replaced by the peculiar disinterest of the aesthetic state. Lipps argues the case for descending incongruity, that is, the modulation in perception when what has been seen as momentous or significant is revealed as insignificant, which theory places him dangerously close to simple superiority theories which he totally rejects: '[Dies gesteigerte Selbstgefühl] ist aber der schlechteste Erklärungsgrund, den man finden kann.'[18] He presents his difference from the commonplace understanding of some form of comparative approach by concentrating exclusively on the receiving subject and rejecting the theories of Groos:

> Eine Art des 'Hereinfallens' gehört zu jeder Komik. Das Komische muß uns in Anspruch nehmen, als ob es mehr wäre, als nur dies komisch Nichtige. Es muß in unseren Augen den Anspruch erheben, mehr zu sein.[19]

And he goes on to define the specific twist he is giving to superiority theories:

> Auch eine 'Überlegenheit' findet bei der Komik statt, nur in völlig anderem als dem Groos'schen Sinne, nämlich eine Überlegenheit meiner Auffassungskraft über ein Aufzufassendes. Und daran schließt sich ein entsprechendes Gefühl,

wenn nicht der 'Überlegenheit', so doch der gelösten Spannung.[20]

But this identification of descending incongruity as perceived by the subject is not only a further instance of an absence of dialectic in the reciprocity between subject and object, it also represents at the end of the nineteenth-century virtually no advance on the famous Kantian dictum concerning the response of laughter, even to the preoccupation with the comic object as nothing: 'Das Lachen ist ein Affekt aus der plötzlichen Verwandlung einer gespannten Erwartung in nichts'.[21] And many decades after Lipps a similar position can still be found in the work of Elder Olson:

> In investigating the nature of the comic, we found that it was not so much a question of laughter as of the restoration of the mind to a certain condition. This, we said, was a pleasant, or rather euphoric condition of freedom from desires and emotions which move men to action, and one in which we were inclined to take nothing seriously and to be gay about everything. The transition to this state was effected through a special kind of relaxation of concern: a katastasis, as I called it, of concern through the annihilation of the concern itself - not by the substitution for desire of its contrary, aversion, nor by the replacement, say, of fear, by the contrary emotion of hope, which is also serious, but by the conversion of the grounds of concern into absolutely nothing.[22]

All three, then, Kant, Lipps and Olson, are concerned with a quantitative change in the degree of concern or involvement as the mechanism whereby psychical energy is both initially created and then rendered superfluous; and that argument is not really advanced by Koestler in *The Act of Creation*:

> The sudden bisociation of an idea or event with
> the two habitually incompatible matrices will
> produce a comic effect, provided that the
> narrative, the semantic pipe-line, carries the right
> kind of emotional tension. When the pipe is
> punctured, and our expectations are fooled, the
> now redundant tension gushes out in laughter, or
> is spilled in the gentler form of the sou-rire.[23]

Olson's definition of the state or condition of mind in which the
perception of the comic should leave the subject, a condition of
freedom from desires and emotions which move men to action, does
indeed represent a 'Null' in respect of determination, that is, the state
of psychical balance which for Schiller is the aesthetic condition. But
in Olson's argument the absence of determination is achieved only on
the basis of an absence of content through 'the annihilation of the
concern itself'. However, in the twentieth Aesthetic Letter cited above
that state of psychical equilibrium can, according to Schiller, be
achieved through the counterbalancing of sensual practical relation by
the perception of form, a dynamic process of oscillation between
'Stoff-' and 'Formtrieb', mobilising that unique condition in which the
'Spieltrieb' is operative. Release from affection, then, can result not
only from a quantitative change in the degree of concern or
involvement that the subject has with the object, but it can also arise
from a qualitative change in relation between the subject and object
due to the interpolation of distance, and equally a qualitative change
within the self:

> It is a difference of outlook due . . . to the
> insertion of Distance. This Distance appears to lie
> between our own self and its affections, using the
> latter term in its broadest sense as anything which
> affects our being, bodily or spiritually, e.g. as
> sensation, perception, emotional state or idea.
> Usually, though not always, it amounts to the
> same thing to say that the Distance lies between

our own self and such objects as are the sources
or vehicles of such affections.[24]

Within the terms of this model two conditions are met which are
central to the present discussion of comedy. First, the term comedy
when applied to literary dramatic works is expressive of an image of
organic form, in which significant patterns and tensions are articulated
and are available for perception. Second, the major stumbling block to
their perception within the appropriate aesthetic mode as crystallised
within the assumed relation underlying the response of laughter,
namely a practical and interested orientation, is susceptible to a
resolution based on Schillerian aesthetics, which both allows for the
presence of the generally accepted conditions for the generation of
laughter, specifically irony, and yet which subsumes these conditions
within a model of what constitutes the aesthetic object and the
aesthetic consciousness.

NOTES

1. *Schillers Sämtliche Schriften*, edited by K. Goedeke, (Stuttgart, 1867ff.), X, 351.
2. S. Langer, *Feeling and Form*, (London, 1953).
3. N. Frye, *Anatomy of Criticism*, (Princeton, 1971).
4. L. Jekels, "On the Psychology of Comedy" in L. J., *Selected Papers*, (London, 1952), pp. 97-104.
5. M. Grotjahn, *Beyond Laughter. Humor and the Subconscious*, (New York, 1957).
6. *Die deutsche Komödie*, edited by W. Hinck, (Düsseldorf, 1977), p. 31.
7. Jekels, op. cit., p. 97.
8. M. G. Ward, "The Comedy of *Weh dem, der lügt!*" in *Essays in Nineteenth Century Austrian Literature*, edited by B. O. Murdoch and M. G. Ward, (Glasgow, 1983), p. 36.
9. W. M. Merchant, *Comedy*, (London, 1972), p. 53: 'There is clearly a related rhythm between the annual pattern of pagan and christian rite: equally clearly comedy echoes this mythic pattern.'

10.	Schiller, X, 460.
11.	Ibid., X, 345.
12.	Ibid., X, 344f.
13.	Ibid., XIV, 9f.
14.	Ibid., XIV, 11.
15.	Ibid.
16.	Ibid., X, 365.
17.	Th. Lipps, *Komik und Humor. Eine psychologisch-ästhetische Untersuchung*, (Hamburg/Leipzig, 1898), p. 141.
18.	Ibid., p. 13.
19.	Ibid., p. 25.
20.	Ibid., p. 27.
21.	I. Kant, *Kritik der Urteilskraft* in I. K., *Sämtliche Werke*, (Leipzig, 1924), VI, 213.
22.	E. Olson, *The Theory of Comedy*, (Bloomington/London, 1968), p. 25.
23.	A. Koestler, *The Act of Creation*, (London, 1969), p. 52.
24.	E. Bullough, "'Psychical Distance' as a Factor in Art and an Aesthetic Principle" in E. B., *Aesthetics*, edited by E. M. Wilkinson, (London, 1951), p. 94.

CHAPTER III

DER ZERBROCHNE KRUG

Considerations such as those outlined in the second chapter of this study might well seem of little relevance to a reading of *Der zerbrochne Krug*,[1] a work which has as its focus an event as ostensibly insignificant as the breaking of a pitcher. And indeed there is much in the play functioning as the trigger for laughter, which arguably speaks against an approach designed to locate the comedy of a work in its significant form, and which rather concentrates on those aspects of the text which seem to invite an interested response, such as that which is invoked by satire. Kleist's use, for example of the stage business of dressing in the second scene could well be interpreted as conveying a judgement on the nature of the judiciary: the office of village judge is one that can be donned and discarded with the ceremonial robes, and is patently not a reality which is coexistent with the incumbent.[2] For the comparative exercise which underlies satire to function - *in nuce* a comparison between the ideal and the real to the latter's disadvantage - there has to be what is tantamount to a sense of complicity between author and audience whereby the author can assume a common opinion to exist independently of the specific text, in this case an expectation of the dignity and probity of the judiciary, against which the realised image, Adam, can be played off in order to create the laughter of mockery and derision.

It is to this questions of this order that Holl turns his attention in the study *Schiller und die Komödie* when he considers Schiller's reflections in the announcement for a comedy prize organised by Goethe and himself in 1800. Schiller expresses regret that in theatrical practice:

> das Interesse noch viel zu sehr aus der Empfindung und aus sittlichen Rührungen geschöpft wird. Das Sittliche aber so wie das Pathetische macht immer ernsthaft und jene geistreiche Heiterkeit und Freiheit des Gemüths, welche in uns hervorzubringen das schöne Ziel der Comödie ist, läßt sich nur durch eine absolute moralische Gleichgültigkeit erreichen . . .[3]

In similar vein Schiller observes in his essay "Tragödie und Komödie":

> Behandelt die Comödie etwas, was unser moralisches Gefühl intereßiert, so liegt ihr ob, es zu neutralisieren, d.i. es in die Klasse natürlicher Dinge zu versetzen, welche nach der Causalität nothwendig erfolgen.[4]

Turning his attention then to *Der zerbrochne Krug* Holl simply states: 'wir sehen, wie ein an sich unmoralischer Stoff durch die Behandlungsweise aus der Sphäre des Moralischen herausgehoben wird',[5] with no indication as to how this transmutation is achieved. In view of the continuing body of opinion which chooses to stress thee satirical-cum-critical dimension of the text, it is in any case questionable whether, in these terms, such a transmutation is achieved. Indeed, when working with the model of comedy suggested in the second chapter of this study, it is fundamentally questionable whether the neutralisation of all practical interest and involvement is either necessary or desirable, a point discussed below in further detail, since a dynamic relationship between audience and text with the latter changing back and fore from interested to disinterested response is the structural base for the necessary ironic relationship and hence the creation of laughter. But whatever specific points for debate arise in this context, the overriding consideration is that moments of satire or farce, like moments of verbal or visual humour, in whatever quantity they may be present in a work, cannot come to constitute an image of living form. That comes alone from the complete 'Gestalt' of the work.

In analysing the status of these aspects of the text, however, there is one recurrent concern in the critical literature which needs to be subjected to sceptical evaluation, and that is the repeated assertion that the moments of obvious humour - the jokes, the stage business, the puns and so forth - have the function, or at least the effect, of casting a gloss of comedy over what is in effect a tragic constellation, and moreover one that is closely allied to Kleist's known tragic vision.[7] Such interpretations of *Der zerbrochne Krug* rely heavily for their rationale on the central scenes dealing with the rift between Eve and Ruprecht. By attributing the failure of human relationships to the absence of that sixth sense of trust which in Kleistian terms can alone act as a guaranteed mediator of truth, the lines:

> Pfui, Ruprecht, pfui, o schäme dich, daß du
> Mir nicht in meiner Tat vertrauen kannst. (ll.1164f.)

or:

> Was ich mit Händen greife, glaub ich gern. (l. 1176)

or again:

> Warum, o Ruprecht, sprich, warum nicht sollt ich
> Auf dein Vertraun hin sagen, daß dus warst? (ll. 1182f.)

seem to play on the familiar theme of Man in a fallen state, cast out, by virtue of his distinguishing feature of consciousness, from the paradise of a naive and reliable contact a reality outside the immediate solipsistic self. The conventional wisdom on Kleist allies that particular recurrent concern to the question of the fallibility of the senses as the media which in conjunction with the reflective or conscious mind repeatedly fail to establish a sure foundation for interpersonal or self/world relations. Such an issue would seem to be raised in Scene 7 where, in Ruprecht's account of the events of the previous evening, the senses of sight and hearing are shown to be inadequate in as much as they give him a false image of the real events; this issue would then seem to be further explored in the translation of Ruprecht's metaphorical blindness into real blindness as the fleeing Adam throws sand into his eyes.

By far the most sensitive and influential account of this dimension of the text was provided as long ago as 1955 in Ilse Graham's analysis "The Broken Pitcher: Hero of Kleist's Comedy"[9] and subsequently reiterated in her study of *Kleist, Word into Flesh*.[10] Working from a detailed explication of Frau Marthe's extensive description of both the pitcher's history and its present appearance, Professor Graham concludes that what Kleist demonstrates in the figure of Frau Marthe is a mind incapable of recognising any reality appertaining to the pitcher other than that of its simple material constitution, which mental attitude can then also be discerned in Ruprecht's obstinate adherence to a reality that is likewise material: 'Was ich mit Händen greife, glaub ich gern'. (l. 1177) The reactions of these two central characters, she goes on to argue, are analogous to the problems experienced by a range of characters across Kleist's total oeuvre, problems that she elsewhere pithily summarises as the dilemma of the 'Fall into a positivistic mode of knowing and the disastrous reverberations of such literalism in the sphere of relationship',[11] citing as supporting evidence the epistemological eschatology of *Über das Marionettentheater*. For Professor Graham, as for so many critics, the fallen state, the existence of Man in that second phase of the ternary development in which 'solche Mißgriffe . . . sind unvermeidlich, seitdem wir vom Baum der Erkenntnis gegessen haben'[12] is symbolically articulated in the broken state of the pitcher; the state of oneness and wholeness has been rent asunder.[13]

Given the conventional resonance of the symbol of a pitcher as mediated through a biblical-cum-folk tradition it is tempting when considering not only the title of the work but also the quasi-theological framework established in the very first scene, complete with references to the first Adam, the Fall, the path of sin, the club foot and so forth, to establish an associative chain in which sexual innocence and the loss of virginity come to exist in parallel with the innocence of Man and the Fall from grace.[14] Certainly the repeated association of Adam with the devil, the potential parallel between his club foot and the cloven hoof of the devil, together with the folk figure of Frau Brigitte would seem to continue the explicit theological background that is suggested by Licht at the beginning in lines such as:

> Ihr stammt doch von einem lockern Ältervater,
> Der so beim Anbeginn der Dinge fiel,
> Und wegen seines Falls berühmt geworden;
> Ihr seid doch nicht -? (ll. 9 - 12)

The most fully developed examination of this aspect of the work is that started by Delbrück in an article in the *Deutsche Vierteljahrsschrift*[15] and then continued in his monograph *Kleists Weg zur Komödie*.[16] But repeatedly in the critical literature statements can be found such as: '. . . what the pitcher in its lamentable state presents and represents is not only a petty domestic quarrel in a Dutch village. Its breakage is a cue for the disruption, an in-two-ness of the large world, of the world at large'.[17] Yet, as I have argued elsewhere, to take the symbolic, or more properly, the potentially symbolic resonance of the work seriously, despite Kleist's obvious invitation to go down such a path, not only in the allusions to the original Fall mentioned above, but also by having the theological analogy directly discussed by the characters of the play in the opening scene, is perhaps to enter a world of unsubstantiated illusion.[18] For there appears to be an insuperable gulf between the realities of the fictional situation and the symbolic superstructure that they are required to support. If on the one hand the broken pitcher suggests a fallen state, in particular a loss of (sexual) innocence, as according to the biblical-cum-folk tradition it should, a central problem arises since nowhere in the dramatic action is it indicated that such a 'fall' has in fact occurred.

In as far as this matter is directly raised in the play it is to the figure of Eve that attention is drawn, with both Frau Marthe and Ruprecht advancing the interpretation that the broken pitcher equates with the loss of Eve's innocence:

> 's der zerbrochne Krug nicht, der sie wurmt,
> Die Hochzeit ist es, die ein Loch bekommen,
> Und mit Gewalt hier denkt sie sie zu flicken.
> Ich aber setze noch den Fuß eins drauf:
> Verflucht bin ich, wenn ich die Metze nehme. (ll. 440 - 4)

> Willst du etwa
> Die Fiedel tragen, Evchen, in der Kirche
> Am nächsten Sonntag reuig Buße tun?
> Dein guter Name lag in diesem Topfe,
> Und vor der Welt mit ihm ward er zerstoßen,
> Wenn auch vor Gott nicht, und vor mir und dir. (ll. 487 - 92)

It is, however, quite clear that Adam's designs on Eve were thwarted and that she remains pure,[19] not only in a sexual sense, but also in the sense that it is she of all the characters in the play who has not fallen into that literalism which characterises the Kleistian epistemological fall, since it is she who retains and represents faith in the intuitive mode of apprehension crystallised in and around the concept of 'Gefühl'.[20] It is true that the final scene ends with a form of literalism in Frau Marthe's demand that justice should be done to her pitcher, but she stands alone here in a scene of reconciliation and forward looking marriage plans. Balance and equilibrium have been restored both to the situation and to those familial relationships which in the course of the work have come under strain; and there is even a promise that, all things being equal, Adam will be reinstated, much to Licht's chagrin. In accordance with the principles of comic dramatic structure the events have come full circle to return to the point before the events of the previous evening, bar one occurrence that cannot be undone, namely the shattering of the pitcher. In terms then of the structuration of the action, in particular in the construction of the end of the text as an effective return to a state of balance and poise that predates the disruption and confusion with which the comic action deals, it is possible to argue for the presence in Kleist's text of those elements that in Chapter II were identified as recurrent patterns within the organic or significant form of comedy. But a full return to the preceding state is not possible in that the damage to the pitcher cannot be undone, as is emphasised by Frau Marthe's absurd demands in the closing scene of the play. The shattering of the pitcher is irreversible, and as such implies at least a change.

If, however, it is accepted, as suggested above, that the traditional connotations of the motif or symbol of the pitcher are incommensurate with the realities of the fictional situation set up by the text, and that they are furthermore clearly irreconcilable with any reading of the text as an articulation of the significant form of comedy, the question still remains as to what the motif may signify.[21] To quote Professor Graham once again, the pitcher, the object after which Kleist names his play albeit under the influence of the Le Veau etching, cannot be regarded as an irrelevance, and any reading of the text that fails to do justice to the 'titular hero' cannot be deemed adequately to cope with the work as a structured whole. Even disregarding Frau Marthe's unequivocal statement: 'Erlaubt! Wie schön der Krug, gehört zur

Sache!' (1.679), a cursory glance at the economy of the text reveals that the pitcher occupies an important position, with a considerable number of lines in Scene 7 being devoted to an elaborate account of its appearance and history, and this is to say nothing of its importance at other moments within the text. Curiously, given the ostensible centrality of the motif of the pitcher, the description of its present state and its seemingly miraculous past has relatively infrequently been seen as of any moment, other than perhaps as a source of humour.[22] Indeed, even in the one analysis of this matter by Professor Graham that can be said to have had any lasting influence on scholarship, it is not the substance of the extensive description of the pitcher that constitutes the focus of interest, but rather the manner of Frau Marthe's description. For all the richness of that particular avenue of approach, it is arguably at least as instructive to consider the substance of the illustrations on the pitcher as well as its subsequent history as narrated in the text, since this yields a reading of the pitcher which would appear not only to relate to the issue of comedy as discussed in the previous two chapters, but also to do so in a way that accords with Kleist's treatment of other symbols in the work.[23]

Both in Heinrich Gessner's idyll 'Der zerbrochene Krug',[24] an adaptation of his father's prose story and a source for Kleist's work, and in Zschokke's story *Der zerbrochene Krug* (for which the Gessner idyll was similarly a source) care is taken to establish precisely the content of the illustrations on the pitcher. In Gessner's idyll what is described is a series of scenes from antiquity: Pan and Syrinx, Europa and Zeus in the form of a bull, and Bacchus. In each of these scenes there is a clear indication of both sexuality and seduction, and consequently in thematic terms each would seem to accord with the traditional symbolic implications of a pitcher in a broken state.

Zschokke's story, dealing with the judge Herr Hautmartin's dubious quest for the beautiful Mariette's favours, contains the following description of the pitcher:

> Sieh nur, der Rand ist strahlendes Gold, und die
> Blumen daran blühen nicht schöner im Garten und
> sind doch nur gemalt. Und in der Mitte das
> Paradies! Sieh doch nur, Mariette, wie die Äpfel
> vom Baume lachen; es gelüstet einem fast. Und
> Adam kann nicht widerstehen, wie ihm die
> hübsche Eva einen zum Kosten darbietet. Und
> sieh doch, wie allerliebst das Lämmchen spielend
> um den alten Tiger hüpft und die schneeweiße
> Taube mit dem gold-grünen Halse vor dem Geier
> dasteht, als wollte sie mit ihm schnäbeln.[25]

and subsequently:

> Als aber Mariette die Scherben des durchlöcherten
> Kruges brachte - als Manon das Paradies verloren
> sah, den guten Adam ohne Kopf und von der Eva
> nur noch die Beine fest stehend; die Schlange
> unverletzt triumphierend, den Tiger unbeschädigt,
> aber das Lämmchen bis auf den Schwanz
> verschwunden, als hätte es der Tiger hinunter-
> geschluckt - da brach Mutter Manon heulend in
> Verwünschungen aus und sagte: "Man sieht's
> wohl, der Wurf kam aus Teufels Hand."[26]

Thus while both the Gessner idyll and the Zschokke story deal with seduction and sexual conquest in terms of their material and have pictorial representations appropriate to their subject matter - in the case of Zschokke, moreover, representations that would have been ideally suited to Kleist's play - Kleist himself has chosen for the central scene on his pitcher a scene from history. Given on the one hand the earthy 'realism' of Kleist's work the deliberate rejection of classical, rococo and other stylised iconographical traditions is perhaps to be expected, but the question remains as to whether the particular scene he has chosen can properly be deemed to bear any further significance.

From Frau Marthe's account it is learnt that represented on the pitcher in *Der zerbrochne Krug* is the abdication of Charles V in favour of his son Philip II, a key event in the history of the

Netherlands. The significance of this episode for the late eighteenth and early nineteenth century can perhaps best be gleaned from the kind of interpretation offered by Schiller in the *Geschichte des Abfalls der vereinigten Niederlande von der Spanischen Regierung*. Having opened his study with a clear statement of interpretative summary:

> Eine der merkwürdigsten Staatsbegebenheiten, die das sechszehnte Jahrhundert zum glänzendsten der Welt gemacht haben, dünkt mir die Gründung der niederländischen Freiheit. Wenn die schimmernden Thaten der Ruhmsucht und einer verderblichen Herrschbegierde auf unsere Bewunderung Anspruch machen, wie vielmehr eine Begebenheit, wo die bedrängte Menschheit um ihre edelsten Rechte ringt, wo mit der guten Sache ungewöhnliche Kräfte sich paaren, und die Hülfsmittel entschloßner Verzweiflung über die furchtbaren Künste der Tiranney in ungleichem Wettkampf siegen. Groß und beruhigend ist der Gedanke, daß gegen die trotzigen Anmaßungen der Fürstengewalt endlich noch eine Hülfe vorhanden ist, daß ihre berechnetsten Pläne an der menschlichen Freiheit zu Schanden werden, daß ein herzhafter Widerstand auch den gestreckten Arm eines Despoten beugen, heldenmüthige Beharrung seine schrecklichen Hülfsquellen endlich erschöpfen kann.[27]

Schiller then goes on to observe of the triadic relationship between Charles V, Philip II and the Flemish peoples:

> Karl verfehlte seine Absicht ganz, da er seinen Sohn den Flämingern vorstellte. Weniger drückend würden sie in der Folge sein Joch gefunden haben, wenn er seinen Fuß nie in ihr Land gesetzt hätte. Aber sein Anblick kündigte es ihnen an; sein Eintritt in Brüssel hatte ihm alle Herzen verloren. Des Kaisers freundliche Hingebung an dies Volk diente jetzt nur dazu, den hochmüthigen Ernst seines Sohns desto

> widriger zu erheben. Nunmehr hatten sie das
> Geschöpf gesehen, von welchem nachher ihre
> Leiden ausgiengen . . . In seinem Angesicht
> hatten sie den verderblichen Anschlag gegen ihre
> Freiheit gelesen, den er schon damals in seiner
> Brust auf und nieder wälzte. Sie waren
> vorbereitet, einen Tirannen in ihm zu finden, und
> gerüstet, ihm zu begegnen.[28]

It is from within this understanding of Philip and his relationship to the Netherlands that not only can parallels to the fictional situation of *Der zerbrochne Krug* be drawn, since there also, albeit on a much reduced scale, it is legitimate to talk of an attempt at the tyrannical manipulation of the people of a village near Utrecht, with the opening stage direction giving a precise geographical location, but also there is embedded in the theme of tyranny and its overthrow the ideological constellation which was identified in Chapter II of this study as an important component of the organic form of comedy. In this context an important indicator as to the significance of the motif of a broken pitcher is to be found in the *Variant*. [29] As Eve explains the motivation for her actions to Walter, she speaks of the exercise of authority by the Spanish over the Netherlands, explicitly defining this as tyranny, and most revealingly employing the word 'zerbrochen' to describe the breaking of tyrannical domination:

> Ihr wißt, daß ein Edikt jüngst ist erschienen,
> Das von je hundert Söhnen jeden Orts
> Zehn für dies Frühjahr zu den Waffen ruft,
> Der rüstigen. Denn der Hispanier
> Versöhnt sich mit dem Niederländer nicht,
> Und die Tyrannenreute will er wieder
> Sich, die zerbrochene, zusammenbinden. (ll. 1959 - 65)

In the four episodes that then follow in Frau Marthe's account, recording the remarkable history of the pitcher, this thematic or ideological constellation is seen to be continued. In the first episode the reference is to the capture of Brill from the Spanish by a group of sea-beggars under Treslong and its establishment as a harbour of refuge in the name of the Prince of Orange, an act which saw the beginnings of the future Dutch republic. The pitcher, which by virtue of the illustration on it is associated with tyrannical domination, emerges from this attack unscathed to be passed down to Fürchtegott, the gravedigger. In this second episode recounting Fürchtegott's marriage at the age of sixty to a girl much younger than himself, there is a strong reminiscence of a stock comic situation of a marriage across the generation gap, but one that Kleist inverts by having the old man survive and the young girl die. In the third episode the associations of the pitcher with both death and domination are continued in the fate of Zachäus who broke his neck while trying to escape from French invaders at Tirlemont (Tienen) in 1635. Once again the pitcher miraculously survives as it finally does the fire of 1666, only to be broken as a wily old judge makes good his escape from the bedroom of a village girl.

On one level it is undeniably the case that Frau Marthe's long account of the pitcher is a ripe source of comic effect in the work. She would appear, for example, to be oblivious to the impossibility of Zachäus' recounting the story of his attempt to escape the French invaders since he was killed in the attempt, or of the absurdity of suggesting that a character depicted on the pitcher should now fall over since the sword on which he was leaning has fallen away with the shattering of the pitcher, and so forth. But to see the significance of these lines as restricted to the creation of comic effect, is to concentrate, as does Professor Graham albeit under the heading of a very different concern, on Frau Marthe as a character and to leave out of account the process of characterisation and definition of the pitcher itself, which is also being conducted here. Bearing in mind the kind of thematic concern which it was argued above can be seen consistently to return in works of comedy and which contributes to the status of the genre as a symbolisation of human experience, the defining context that Kleist establishes for the pitcher through Frau Marthe would appear to be carefully controlled. By virtue of the illustrations on it the pitcher functions as a symbol of domination and tyranny, a symbol of the way in which the exercise of power inhibits freedom.[30] Further, in the story of Fürchtegott the relations within the power axis are articulated to generation groupings. In the two events from the pitcher's past where attempts were made to escape domination, Brill and Tirlemont, the pitcher has remained intact.[31] Yet now it is broken in the context of an action where the abuse of power on Adam's part has been thwarted, and indeed it is broken at precisely the very moment of its being thwarted by the individual who is defeated and eventually unmasked as the abuser of power, namely Adam.

From these circumstances, then, it can be argued that the central motif of the pitcher needs to be subjected to a fundamental revision vis-a-vis the commonplace assumptions held about it. Most importantly, this revision requires a thoroughgoing reassessment of the values that have conventionally been seen as attached to a pitcher, and in particular a broken pitcher. Whereas when drawing on a traditional framework of reference for the symbol of a pitcher the clear invitation is present to see it in its broken state as something negative, as a symbol of the loss of innocence, whether that innocence be sexual, epistemological or indeed theological, the defining context that Kleist has set up necessitates an inversion of that value judgement. If the pitcher is taken as representing restriction, imposed authority and indeed a tyrannical power structure, then its breaking becomes a very positive occurrence, and a concentrated articulation of the comic 'Gestalt' of the work.

There is, however, one further ramification from Frau Marthe's account of the pitcher that derives from the manner of her relationship to the pitcher, from her inability to distinguish between the different dimensions of the pitcher and her obstinate clinging to its material reality. For the problems of differentiated perception, or rather the absence of differentiated perception is raised elsewhere in the text, and moreover in such a way as to cope with the nagging sense of unease underlying much analysis of the work which argues that at root what Kleist has presented us with is essentially a tragedy, a tragic constellation familiar from his other works over which a comic veneer has been laid. Frau Marthe is not the only character who betrays an inability to relate to the world outside themselves on anything other than a literal empirical level.

In the Scene 9 Eve delivers an impassioned speech imploring Ruprecht in his relationship with her to rely on trust and feeling, motifs very familiar from the main corpus of Kleist's writing, even to the point of allowing himself to be named as the guilty party (ll.1162ff.). Reluctantly Ruprecht agrees to be named if Eve thinks that she can thereby spare herself the shame of the stocks, the punishment for lax morality, and in this agreement he betrays his belief in her infidelity. A large measure of the significance of this episode derives from Ruprecht's bald statement already cited above: 'Was ich mit Händen greife, glaub ich gern'. Faith, by definition 'the substance of things hoped for, the evidence of things not seen' (*Hebrews*, XI, i), is something that Ruprecht willingly accords only to that which is tangible. In its insistence on tactile relations with reality, and the consequently implied passive role of the percipient in the act of perception, this contradictory assertions of Ruprecht's is, however, a continuation of a more protracted debate being conducted in the work about modes and manners of perception.

In Scene 7 when recounting his experience of the events of the previous evening Ruprecht develops what is for him a remarkable degree of articulacy, and, consonant with the sense of drama and immediacy created by his use of the historic present, he personifies the senses of sight and hearing to suggest the urgency with which he attempted to discern what was actually happening:

> Drauf - wie ich übern Lindengang mich näh're
> Bei Marthens, wo die Reihen dicht gewölbt,
> Und dunkel, wie der Dom zu Utrecht, sind,
> Hör ich die Gartentüre fernher knarren.
> Sieh da! Da ist die Eve noch! sag ich,
> Und schicke freudig Euch, von wo die Ohren
> Mir Kundschaft brachten, meine Augen nach -
> - Und schelte sie, da sie mir wiederkommen,
> Für blind, und schicke auf der Stelle sie
> Zum zweitenmal, sich besser umzusehen,
> Und schimpfe sie nichtswürdige Verleumder,
> Aufhetzer, niederträchtge Ohrenbläser,
> Und schicke sie zum drittenmal, und denke,
> Sie werden, weil sie ihre Pflicht getan,
> Unwillig los sich aus dem Kopf mir reißen,
> Und sich in einen andern Dienst begeben:
> Die Eve ists, am Latz erkenn ich sie,
> Und einer ists noch obenein. (ll. 899 - 916)

One reading of this speech is to see in it an example of Kleist's recurrent concern with the fallibility of the senses as the media which in conjunction with the reflective or conscious mind repeatedly fail to establish reliable perception of reality. It is after all through an analogy centred on the sense of sight that Kleist's records the impact of Kantian, or the so-called recent Kantian philosophy on himself. And this motif is then continued when what is here his metaphorical blindness is translated into literal blindness as the fleeing Adam throws sand in his eyes. But it is questionable whether the resonance of Ruprecht's speech and the striking personification as well as the conversion of the remote senses of sight and hearing into quasi-tactile senses is limited to a reworking or further exemplification of the familiar problematic of Kleist's oeuvre.

The idea of a hierarchy of senses has a long philosophical tradition, as does the linking of the sense of sight to aesthetic perception. The eighteenth century in particular had constant recourse in epistemological discussion to the connection between knowledge and visual stimulation; hence also the recurrent preoccupation at the time with the problem of blindness. Sight, however, does not stand alone as the higher sense, but is also set alongside hearing as the two senses which are distant from their object of perception and consequently do not rely on direct or unmediated impression. It is in the XVI Aesthetic Letter that Schiller not only makes this particular distinction, but establishes 'the physical basis (he means it as more than mere analogy) of the aesthetic phenomena of "semblance" and "distance" in optical illusions and in the actual distance of objects from the organs of sense in visual and aural perception':[32]

> Die Natur selbst ist es, die den Menschen von der Realität zum Scheine emporhebt, indem sie ihn mit zwey Sinnen ausrüstete, die ihn bloß durch den Schein zur Erkenntnis des Wirklichen führen. In dem Auge und dem Ohr ist die andringende Materie schon hinweggewälzt von den Sinnen, und das Objekt entfernt sich von uns, das wir in den thierischen Sinnen unmittelbar berühren. Was wir durch das Auge sehen, ist von dem verschieden, was wir empfinden, denn der Verstand springt über das Licht hinaus zu den Gegenständen. Der Gegenstand des Takts ist eine Gewalt, die wir erleiden; der Gegenstand des Auges und des Ohrs ist eine Form, die wir erzeugen. Solange der Mensch noch ein Wilder ist, genießt er bloß mit den Sinnen des Gefühls, denen die Sinne des Scheins in dieser Periode bloß dienen. Er erhebt sich entweder gar nicht zum Sehen, oder er befriedigt sich doch nicht mit demselben. Sobald er anfängt, mit dem Auge zu genießen, und das Sehen für ihn einen selbstständigen Werth erlangt, so ist er auch schon ästhetisch frey, und der Spieltrieb hat sich entfaltet.[33]

The context in which the senses of sight and hearing are raised in Ruprecht's account makes it clear that to allow these senses to operate in this quasi-tactile way is to be lured into a false perception and misinterpretation of reality. But, according at least to Schiller's understanding, these senses can be viewed as those which, by virtue of their distanced relationship to the object of perception, condition not only a different relation of perception from the lower senses, but a relation which, at least potentially, is aesthetic in constitution. On the basis of the long tradition of debate on the nature of these senses, on which Schiller is drawing, it could be argued that what is being raised within the play in the figures of Frau Marthe and Ruprecht is an issue ranging beyond any immediate concerns dictated by plot and dramatic action. In particular it can be seen as an issue which touches on the matter of aesthetics, specifically the question of the distanced relationship to material that is appropriate and necessary for aesthetic perception, the perception of significant permanent form through the transitory. It is perhaps not fortuitous that the two non-tactile and remote senses that Schiller discusses, sight and hearing, are precisely those used by a theatre audience. Just as Ruprecht and others in the work misapprehend reality, with the misapprehension characterised as a result of their failure to allow their senses to operate in an appropriate mode, so there is an implicit injunction through this to the audience to relate to the material in such a way that the direct affection resulting from unmediated contact should be qualitatively modified in order to allow the character of the material as illusion, 'Schein', to become apparent. Then the audience is in a position to perceive in the material, or rather through the material, the patterns and tensions, the significant form, which is embodied in and yet transcends the localised and immediate dramatic constellation.

In particular this bears on the matter of how those moments in the text should be interpreted, that approximate to the tragic scenario to be found in other of Kleist's works; those moments when misunderstanding and confusion put under strain the relations between lovers, mother and daughter, father and son, and when the audience is drawn into the text to share the emotions of suffering, despair and anger. Distance is required to allow those moments to form not discrete units of meaning in which capacity the audience would relate to them in a condition of passive affection and to their tragic potential, but rather to constitute component parts within the organic form of comic structuration.[34] In that latter capacity they are then seen not as discrete but as subordinate units, which serve both the creation of an image of organic form and the generation of laughter in very precise and controlled ways. Thus the moments when the audience is, as it were, drawn into the text are those at which the desired resolution to the love relationship between Eve and Ruprecht is threatened by the parental figures of the figures of authority. It is at these moments that the psychical energy is generated that can then be dispelled in laughter as the threat is nullified, not by being dissolved or dispelled, but by being neutralised as it comes to be seen in a qualitatively different, i.e. disinterested, light as a constituent element in the greater image of comic form that is the entire play.

Yet there is a very real sense in which Kleist would seem deliberately to have set out to frustrate such an aim. Even the obvious unreality of dramatic action which the dramatist has at his disposal, the facility of partial selection and illumination of events and in particular the control over fictional and real time, is here surrendered as the fictional time occupied by events on stage is made co-existent with the time of the presence of the audience in the theatre. The fictional world that Kleist creates for *Der zerbrochne Krug* is one that is recognisably ordinary and one in which, even allowing for the verse form of iambic pentameters, the language is suffused with the idiom of everyday speech. Above all, it is a fictional world in which the most fundamental of human bonds, primary familial relationships, are seen to come under stress, not in the mediated context of a remote social setting, but rather in a world that is remorselessly mundane.[35]

Within that setting Kleist presents a drama that is in one sense of a traditional type, in that it is characterised by change and development in interpersonal relationships and dramatic situation. More significantly, the movement in the two spheres of relationships and situation in the dramatic configuration would seem to tend towards tragic development and conclusion as mistrust and suspicion, recrimination and accusation, begin to spread. Most obviously, it has been argued, that tendency towards tragic development is counteracted by the extensive use of dramatic irony: the reassuring presence of a figure such as Walter, of whom it is intimated at an early stage that he has a keen eye for malpractice. Equally, there are other ways in which a note of reassurance is conveyed, as, for example, in the prefiguration of events in Adam's dream; the indication of the inconsequentiality of this fictional world that is indicated by the tale of the judge who hanged himself but is brought back to life; the suggestion through Adam's involuntary exclamation: 'Die werden mich doch nicht bei mir verklagen' of the archetypal comic situation of the 'voleur volé' - all these serve to communicate to the audience the probability of a happy ending, and hence they all serve to direct the audience's attention to a concern not so much with what will happen, but rather a concern with how that end will be achieved.

Added to all these aspects of the work there is also the kind of reassurance that derives from Kleist's use of the analytic technique of dramatic construction. By locating the central event of the action, Adam's abortive attempt to seduce Eve, on the evening prior to the events of the dramatic action proper, that is by making the truth of who is the guilty party and what actually happened independent of any change or development in the present dramatic action, Kleist is able to indicate that the movement in the play along potentially tragic lines is a false development. As the characters lapse further and further into misunderstanding and with the misunderstanding growing suspicion and recrimination, the audience becomes increasingly aware of the falsity of this development and increasingly anxious for a resolution based not on new positions and understandings reached by the characters, but on the basis of the revelation of an immutable truth that is fixed unalterably in the past.[36]

Martini,[37] and in his wake Reh,[38] locate the structuring principle provoking a comic response, both in this particular work and in comedy in general, in the fluctuation between, on the one hand, an interested and involved relation to the work, the kind of empathetic relation consequent on those aspects of the action that communicate a sense of the potential tragedy of the situation, and, on the other, a more distanced awareness and appreciation of the illusory and temporary nature of that strand of the action that abounds with confusion and the latent sense of potential tragedy. Such an ironic perspective may arguably account for one aspect of the humorous effect of *Der zerbrochne Krug*. Whereas the audience is aware from an early stage of the truth concerning Adam, Eve and Ruprecht and the circumstances surrounding the breaking of the pitcher, the elucidation of that truth in the fictional world of the drama is repeatedly delayed, so much so that even Walter is momentarily shaken in his conviction of Adam's guilt. It is then at the point where truth and illusion are at their most divergent, that is the point at which Adam arbitrarily condemns Ruprecht and at which the audience experiences the greatest tension arising from the discrepancy between their perception of events and the situation achieved in the dramatic fiction, that Eve breaks her silence, reveals the truth and thereby creates the conditions for the traditional rapid conclusion of a comedy. And in true comic fashion the audience is returned to an inconsequential world: there never was a seduction but merely an abortive attempt, and as with the judge who is miraculously brought back to life, punishment is not absolute - Adam is to be suspended but not dismissed from office.

It is clear from the repeated use of concepts like 'Schein' and 'Spiel' and from the guiding observation that an analysis of the comic involves 'ein poetologisches Problem' centring on 'die Bedeutung einer konstanten Strukturbestimmung der Komödie oder des Lustspiels',[39] that Martini is striving for an understanding of the comic which allows for its assimilation into a theory of the aesthetic such as exists within the idealist tradition. In this respect his enquiry is a welcome departure from the dominant concerns of historically or thematically oriented enquiries. Even more fruitful is Martini's recognition of a dialectical interaction between audience and work in the comic mode, which derives from the repeated alternation between 'Betroffenheit' and 'Distanzierung'. However, the conflation of 'Distanzierung' and 'Überlegenheit' in Martini's argument tends back to the familiar contention that the release or relief which attend the close or other moments of a comic work, the assertion of harmony and balance and the dissolution of threat and obstacles to such harmony and balance, belatedly confirms that perception of events which the audience has in advance seen as appropriate.

That such a model of comic structure, with whatever refinements, necessarily remains tied to the tradition of comic analysis which places at its centre the rhetorical figure of incongruity is inevitable since the audience's dual and alternating relation to the work - 'Betroffenheit' and 'Überlegenheit' - can only create the conditions for dramatic irony. For all the differences in the substance of what is perceived or related to, the two perceptions or relations remain qualitatively the same, both engaging with the work on the level of material interest. The comparative exercise necessary for the realisation of incongruity assumes work and recipient to exist in the same mode; there is, in other words, an equation between the semblance of reality created by the fictional work and the real world inhabited by the audience, whereby the two become co-existent. The irony thus operates within the framework of a relation between audience and work, from which the interpolation of aesthetic distance is precluded, and hence also the possibility of a response incorporating aesthetic freedom.[40]

Within the terms of the theory of the aesthetic and of the model of comedy outlined in the first two chapters of this study, then, a reading of the comedy of *Der zerbrochne Krug* which draws on the motive force of dramatic irony is inadequate, since by necessarily assuming the involvement of direct and practical interest on the part of the audience to be a final cause in the perception of the 'Gehalt' of a work, the vital transmutation of material into form can never be effected. And more immediately, such a reading is inadequate since the model on which the assumptions regarding the operation of dramatic irony are based, fails to recognise the complex structuring of the action, which informs and sustains the significant form of the work. For while it is true that on one level the action of *Der zerbrochne Krug* does intimate an essentially linear development in which the confusion experienced by the characters and their distance from the truth become ever greater to the point where even Walter is forced to doubt his own certainty, and while it is true that this development is increasingly recognised by the audience as erroneous, a contrary movement to that linear thrust is also present as a function of the analytic structure. That contrary movement, deriving simply from the choice of the courtroom as a setting, serves to counteract the linear dimension of the plot, and in that counteraction to establish a significant pattern.

The choice of a legal enquiry as the pretext for the dramatic action of *Der zerbrochne Krug* predetermines to a large extent the possible forms that the action can take. Within the logic of the dramatic fiction the rationale for the characters' presence on stage consists solely in their function as interested parties or witnesses in a court case. Moreover the action does approximate, with whatever digressions and absurdities, to the hearing of a case with the sequential presentation of evidence and questioning of witnesses. Thus Kleist has adopted an external structure which is both additive and episodic. The tendency towards fragmentation which is inherent in that structure is balanced by developing a dialogue which is not tied to the formal procedure of question and answer between a court official and a witness, but which proceeds more freely as a semi-formal argument or debate amongst the characters.[41] Continuity is ensured by loose

73

adherence, appropriate to the situation, to the logic of elimination. Starting from the attempt to ascertain the truth of the events of the previous evening, which however wayward in its adherence to correct procedure and however erroneous its findings, does at least pay lip-service to the method of factual elucidation, the characters become increasingly embroiled in random and even absurd hypothesis. Thus faced with Ruprecht's denial of guilt and with the factual impossibility of Lebrecht's guilt, the red herrings of an intended elopement and the involvement of the devil are introduced. But such movement into patent falsehood and superstition does not proceed under its own momentum nor without deliberate manipulation. With the albeit unwitting assistance of Frau Marthe, Veit, and for a while even Ruprecht, it is Adam who directly or indirectly engineers the increasing divergence from the truth. To ensure the suppression of the truth Adam, with his remarkable ability to think on his feet, is pushed into a series of tactical diversions and counter-moves which are necessitated by the recalcitrance and resistance to confusion, whether intentional or not, which are shown by Eve and Ruprecht.

In one sense those circumstances would seem to invite the application of Bergson's definition of the comic resource as 'Du mécanique plaqué sur du vivant'.[42] The rigidity of Adam's persistence in the role of innocent on the face of a body of evidence which increasingly points to him as the culprit invites the perception of Bergsonian incongruity. But what is much more significant in the development of this dramatic configuration is the presentation of the rifts in relationships in the work along the lines of oppositions across the axes of generation, power and authority. More specifically, these are rifts created by the individual in the play who enjoys within the local community the ultimate power. This is not to play down the seriousness of the threat to the relationship between Eve and Ruprecht, but it is simply to recognise that the threat arises from the machinations of Adam whose activity from beginning to end has the aim of obfuscation.

The motif of blindness, the form of a legal enquiry and the resulting adoption of a broadly analytic dramatic technique are aspects of *Der zerbrochne Krug* which, amongst others, have been related to Sophocles' *Oedipus Rex*.[43] But whereas in the latter play the weighty themes of incest, guilt and punishment are centred on the representative of the younger generation, in *Der zerbrochne Krug* the orientation is reversed. It has, for example, been observed that the relationship between Adam and Eve is close to that of father and daughter, which would signify a double dislocation of the Oedipal complex by both the inversion of the generation axis and the transference of the incest motif from mother/son to father/daughter. In addition biblical tradition is reversed here by making Adam the (unsuccessful) seducer and not the seduced. Both Jekels and Grotjahn have recognised the importance of inversion of the Oedipal pattern for a definition of the comic impulse. Jekels summarises his conclusion: 'the feeling of guilt which, in tragedy, rests upon the son, appears in comedy displaced on the father; it is the father who is guilty',[44] and the specific form of his guilt is to have disturbed a love relationship. The significance of any such principle of inversion either in *Der zerbrochne Krug* or in comedy in general, does not lie in the potential function it might have as parody or caricature of a dominant, that is the perception in the Oedipus situation of 'the genuine meaning of all great human tragedy'.[45] Rather what is involved in the reversal of the Oedipus situation is the creation of an independent image of organic or significant form.[46]

Although she is constrained by her concern for Ruprecht's putative fate as a conscript, Eve refutes as best she can the imputations made by her mother and Adam that Ruprecht is the guilty party. In doing this, she succeeds in confounding the former's attempts to shift the blame from himself onto Ruprecht, and at the same time she denies any doubt that may be cast on her honour. In this rebuttal she finds an

75

ally in the figure of Ruprecht, who not only protests his own innocence but who also, despite his earlier suggestion of Lebrecht as the guilty party, goes on to furnish Lebrecht with a water-tight alibi. More than this, under questioning by Walter in Sc.10, Ruprecht provides certain details of the events of the previous evening which firmly point to Adam as the intruder. And just as Eve is forced to oppose her mother's allegations of impropriety, so Ruprecht gives an unqualified rejection of his father's suspicions of intended elopement.

What then is created in this comedy is a complex build-up of related patterns. In terms of the work as a whole what is enacted is the defeat of Adam's attempts to retain a hold over Eve and to have Ruprecht blamed for his, Adam's, crime. That defeat carries with it the nullification of Frau Marthe's doubts regarding her daughter's honour and Veit's suspicions regarding an intended elopement. The defeat is accomplished by Eve and Ruprecht, who, for all the strain put on the relationship between them, in practice put up a united front of opposition against their elders. The tendency towards polarisation along the lines of generation is highlighted by the part played by Walter, the representative of impartial justice, whose asides to Adam and questions of the other characters would seem to indicate his full possession of the truth, but who has to wait for Eve's explicit condemnation of Adam before he can act.

For a great number of critics, Walter represents something of a *deus ex machina* figure, not only embodying a reassuring presence on stage, but also playing a dominant role in effecting the resolution.[47] In other words, the potential symbolism inherent in his name, by virtue of which he acquires an almost god-like status as the counterpart to the diabolic figure of Adam, has been taken seriously.[48] However, in view of the way in which Kleist has frustrated and inverted other potential symbols in the work, it should also be considered whether a similar technique of reversal is being practiced here. Crucial to this aspect of Walter's significance are the events of the latter part of Scene 10.

Throughout the course of the previous scenes it is clearly conveyed that Walter's suspicions concerning Adam's guilt have not only been growing, but have increasingly been confirmed by the material evidence against Adam. Walter has intervened to stop Adam's attempts to adjourn the court proceedings; he has established that the number of blows Adam has received on the head corresponds to the number of blows delivered by Ruprecht on the intruder as he made good his escape from Eve's bedroom; he has further established that the wall outside Eve's room is covered by a trellis on which is growing a vine, and this would account for the scratches on Adam's face; and he has adopted the strategy of trying to catch Adam in the act of lying. Yet, on a couple of points, it emerges, Adam has told the truth, and this leads initially to Walter's doubt:

Hm! Sollt ich auch dem Manne wohl - (l. 1581)

where he is forced to consider whether he has done Adam an injustice in entertaining suspicions of him, and thence to the significant stage direction to l. 1594, 'verwirrt', when it emerges that Adam's claim not to have visited Frau Marthe's house during the previous nine weeks is true. The state of 'Verwirrung' is familiar from Kleist's other works, and is used to mark the inner disorientation and confusion into which characters are plunged when their inner convictions and the external truth, or appearance of truth, are totally divergent.

The events of Scene 11 again confirm the overwhelming likelihood of Adam's guilt, and with the growing certainty comes growing impatience on Walter's part. But crucially it is not Walter who acts to unmask and defeat Adam. It may be that in allowing Adam, even encouraging him to proceed in his arbitrary way, Walter is carefully manipulating events and bringing matters to a head, but the upshot is that it is Eve who finally utters the words that signal the discomfiture and defeat of Adam. In terms of the significant form that the genre of comedy may project, it is vital that the arbitrary authority exercised by Adam, the static and restrictive domination of the older generation over the younger, should be defeated by the vitality and 'livingness' of youth.[49]

Moreover that final defeat and resolution is anticipated and retrospectively reflected in the series of analogous defeats which constitute the episodic development of the plot and which necessitate the diversions and counter-moves to which Adam has to resort as Eve and Ruprecht successively reject the accusations made against them.[50] Thus, for example, in Scenes 6 and 7 Eve comes under considerable pressure, initially from her mother who considers that Eve has brought dishonour on the family, and subsequently from Adam with the threats regarding Ruprecht's fate following his conscription.[51] Frau Marthe and Adam then enter a kind of alliance as she accuses Ruprecht and Adam seizes the opportunity to condemn Ruprecht and, of course, divert suspicion from himself. That condemnation is then followed by the extensive description of the appearance of the appearance and history of the pitcher, which at the moment of its conclusion leads back into the present of the dramatic action and a further accusation by Frau Marthe against Ruprecht. Following Frau Marthe's account of the events of the previous evening there is yet a further accusation against Ruprecht, which is strenuously denied, for their different reasons, by both Ruprecht and Eve. As Frau Marthe then starts to retreat, Adam once again takes up his threatening stance towards Eve. Throughout these scenes the attitudes struck and actions taken by the characters involved are explicable in terms of their motivation deriving from their position within the immediate circumstances of the dramatic situation; Frau Marthe is convinced of Ruprecht's guilt and responds accordingly: Adam is only to keen to find a culprit for his own crimes: Ruprecht knows it was not he who broke the pitcher: and Eve is torn between a desire to protect Ruprecht and a desire to preserve her own reputation. Yet at the same time, under a more symbolic heading, the immediate dramatic action is yielding a pattern of significant tensions and forces as the conflict splits down the line of a generation axis with Adam and Frau Marthe in opposition to Eve and Ruprecht, and with the bullying tactics of the former group culminating in the assessment offered by Walter:

> Von eurer Aufführung, Herr Richter Adam,
> Weiß ich nicht, was ich denken soll. Wenn ihr selbst
> Den Krug zerschlagen hättet, könntet Ihr
> Von Euch ab den Verdacht nicht eifriger
> Hinwälzen auf den jungen Mann, als jetzt. - (ll. 820 - 4)

Whereas up until this point it has been Eve who has stood at the centre of the attack, the focus now changes to Ruprecht. Just as he had adopted a threatening stance towards Eve, so Adam now directs his authoritarian arbitrariness towards Ruprecht:

> Getraut Er sich
> Etwas dagegen aufzubringen, was?
> Bekennt Er, oder unterfängt Er sich,
> Hier wie ein gottvergeßner Mensch zu leugnen? (ll. 850 - 3)

As Ruprecht's account proceeds, the red herring of Lebrecht as a possible culprit is introduced, once more inspiring hope in Adam, but just as the section in which Eve was under threat culminated in Walter's statement pointing the finger towards Adam, so the section in which Ruprecht is to the fore ends up with an accumulation of evidence against Adam. At this point within the action, however, where Ruprecht has already characterised his eyes as blind and where he recounts how sand was thrown in his face blinding him, he is not in a position to make those connections that would allow him to perceive Adam as the guilty party. Nevertheless, the underlying pattern of conflict and the unconscious opposition mounted by the young lovers against those whose authority is working against their interests is here maintained.

At the beginning of Scene 9, the circumstances are not dissimilar from those at the beginning of Scene 7. Once again Eve is at the centre of the action and under direct threat from Adam, who is quickly joined by Frau Marthe in exerting pressure on her, and once again she resists the pressure, firstly by stating categorically that it was not Ruprecht who broke the pitcher, and then by counteracting the red herring of Lebrecht as the guilty party. In this latter refutation she is quickly joined by Ruprecht, establishing once again the alliance of forces at the heart of the conflict. As on the previous occasion the focus now changes to Ruprecht with the introduction of the idea that he intended to elope with Eve in order to avoid conscription. To sustain the momentum new figures have to be brought into the complex at this point, and the new alliance is that of Veit and Frau Brigitte, and in the same way that relations between mother and daughter have now reached an impasse, so the relations between father and son are shown at the extreme of breaking.

Following Frau Brigitte's arrival and a further chance to incriminate Ruprecht over the matter of the wig, the material evidence accumulates that points conclusively to Adam as the intruder in Eve's bedroom. Indeed so clear are the indications that even Ruprecht sees the truth, underlining his the change in his perception by an explicit statement that he will not on this occasion be blinded. With that realisation on Ruprecht's part, the opposition has reached its climax as Eve and Ruprecht with mutual understanding can provide united resistance to Adam's power. As Adam exercises that power in its most arbitrary way by condemning Ruprecht in the face of all the evidence pointing to himself, Eve breaks her silence, names him, and with the act of naming triumphs over him. In a series of episodes, then, Eve and Ruprecht, now singly, now together, have fought back against Frau Marthe, Veit and above all Adam, whose combined actions have threatened their happiness and their love.[52]

Furthermore, the series of defeats that the young lovers have succeeded in inflicting throughout the course of the drama, which may be seen as refractions and anticipations of the overall victory that they achieve, is analogous to the one central defeat which Adam had suffered the previous evening when Ruprecht's intervention frustrated his designs on Eve. Here again the significance of the pitcher as a negative symbol of authority, whose breaking is a positive occurrence, becomes important. In the *Variant*, Eve recounts that when Adam visited her the previous evening, he removed his wig and hung it on the pitcher. As Ruprecht arrives and Adam beats a hasty retreat, Adam snatches the wig from the pitcher which then falls and breaks. The account of these circumstances underlines the connections made between the pitcher and the motif of authority, which authority is clearly embodied in the wig as a symbol of office. That the pitcher is then broken at precisely the moment when Adam's designs on Eve are thwarted, serves to reinforce the thematic complex of the triumph of love and youth of authority and age. The ultimate triumph of love and the routing of those forces that would oppose it, or in other words the defeat of the elders at the hands of the young lovers, receives its confirmation in the forthcoming marriage of Eve and Ruprecht, significantly arranged for the time of the Pentecost.[53] The tactical flexibility of the Christian calendar in assimilating pagan festivals extends to Whitsun which was in origin a springtime festival celebrating the resurgence of natural life and the first fruits of the new season.[54] That seasonal location of the wedding with the implicit contrast to the snows presently on the ground in Huisum, can be seen as corresponding to the generational grouping of the characters and the conflict.

While, then, at the conclusion of the work, with the restoration of the love relationship between Eve and Ruprecht, the audience can experience the sense of release central to the comic experience, that release is not so much a function of the nullification of the threat to their love - that which is explored in the potentially tragic development of their relationship as authority and power distorts and frustrates it - in quantitative terms. That is to say it is not so much that the threat to them is simply dispelled, but rather it is nullified as a result of being seen in a qualitatively different light. The nature of the threat is no longer perceived as an autonomous force within a dramatic constellation, but is now contained within, and is subservient to, the broad and symbolic structure that is the pattern of significant tensions at the heart of the comic form. The direct involvement with and empathetic relation to the figures of Eve and Ruprecht into which the audience has repeatedly been drawn, can now yield to the aesthetically distanced relation in which the threat is apprehended as a constituent element of the comic symbolisation of human experience.[55]

NOTES

1. All references are to Heinrich von Kleist, *Sämtliche Werke und Briefe*, edited by H. Sembdner, (München, 1961). The text of *Der zerbrochne Krug* is to be found in Vol. I, 175 - 244.
2. That kind of reading is categorically rejected by F. Martini, "Kleist. 'Der zerbrochene Krug': Bauformen des Lustspiels", *Jahrbuch der deutschen Schiller Gesellschaft*, 9 (1965), 379: ' . . . es im *Zerbrochenen Krug* nicht um eine gesellschaftliche Satire geht, die etwa auf den Mißbrauch, die Korruption des Richteramtes mit deren sozialen Konsequenzen zielt . . .'
3. *Schillers Sämtliche Schriften*, edited by K. Goedeke, (Stuttgart, 1867ff.), X, 539.
4. Ibid., X, 543.
5. K. Holl, *Schiller und die Komödie*, (Leipzig, 1925), p. 6.
6. Cf Martini, op. cit., 388, who maintains that as a result of the construction of the work as an image of play, with its illusory constitution constantly reinforced, the relationship between audience and work is not based at all on affection: 'Denn es geht in dem Dorfrichter zu Huisum nicht um einen <realen> Charakter, über dessen Wirkungen im Theaterspielwerk

Sympathien oder Antipathien entscheiden, sondern es geht um eine Spielfigur, die sich in der Kunst ihres <Spielens> innerhalb des Spiels voll entfaltet und derart das Spielvergnügen des Zuschauers anzieht.'

7.   See, as a representative example, J. Gearey, *Heinrich von Kleist. A Study in Tragedy and Anxiety*, (Pennsylvania, 1968), p. 85: 'His tragic sense of life, even in this escapade in a Dutch village, would somehow out.'

8.   See W. Müller-Seidel, *Versehen und Erkennen*, (Köln/Graz, 1961), p. 116: 'Die Ansätze zum Tragischen wurden damit verdrängt; allenfalls im Verhältnis von Eve und Ruprecht sind sie im Motiv des Vertrauens enthalten.' See also H. Reske, *Traum und Wirklichkeit im Werke Heinrich von Kleists*, (Stuttgart, 1969), pp. 73f., and H. J. Schrimpf, "Tragedy and Comedy in the Works of Heinrich von Kleist", *Monatshefte*, 58 (1966), 202f.: 'We hesitate, however, to call tragic that which tinges the comic features in Kleist's *Der zerbrochne Krug* with anxiety. The relationship between Eve and Ruprecht suggests the possibility of a tragic outcome. But this element does not strike us as sufficiently prominent in the comedy as a whole to warrant the label: tragic .'

9.   I. Appelbaum-Graham, "The Broken Pitcher: Hero of Kleist's Comedy", *MLQ*, (16, 1955), 99 - 113.

10.   I. Graham, *Heinrich von Kleist. Word into Flesh: A Poet's Quest for the Symbol*, (Berlin/New York, 1977), pp. 27 - 41.

11.   I. Graham, "Heinrich von Kleist: The Captive Vision", *GQ*, 51 (1978), 3.

12.   Kleist, 'Über das Marionettentheater', II, 342.

13.   This prevalent perception finds a curious inversion in K. Holl, *Geschichte des deutschen Lustspiels*, (Leipzig, 1923), p. 237, where he argues that the figures of Adam and Eve have to be seen as a kind of parallel to the marionette, characterised by a naive grace and inner sureness: 'Die Namenwahl Adam und Eve ist nicht nur die komische Hindeutung auf den Sündenfall, sie weist auch darauf hin, daß hier noch zwei ursprüngliche, naive Menschen vor uns stehen, deren Handeln nicht erkenntnismäßig, sondern triebhaft bestimmt ist.'

14.   See, for example, H. J. Schrimpf, "Kleist. Der zerbrochene Krug" in *Das deutsche Drama*, I, edited by B. von Wiese, (Düsseldorf, 1958), p. 362: 'Hier sind neben der individuellen Wahrheit der allein im innersten Gefühl sich selbst findenden Seele die entblößte generische Kreatürlichkeit und Endlichkeit, die mit dem "Adamsfall" gegebene Fehlbarkeit und Erbärmlichkeit als Wesen des Menschen begriffen.'

15. H. Delbrück, "Zur dramentypologischen Funktion von Sündenfall und Rechtfertigung in Kleists 'Zerbrochenem Krug'", *DVjs*, 45 (1971), 705 - 756.

16. H. Delbrück, *Kleists Weg zur Komödie. Untersuchungen zur Stellung des 'Zerbrochenen Krugs' in einer Typologie des Lustspiels*, (Tübingen, 1974).

17. O. Seidlin, "What the Bell Tolls in Kleist's *Der zerbrochne Krug*', *DVjs*, 51 (1977), 88f. See also L. Hoverland, "Adam und Frau Marthe: polare Verfahrensweisen in Kleists *Der zerbrochne Krug*" in *Heinrich von Kleist-Studien*, edited by A. Ugrinsky, (Berlin, 1980), p. 59: 'Der mit dem Fall gemeinte Verlust einer früheren Ganzheit, Einheit und Selbstverständlichkeit wurde von diesen Interpreten treffend erkannt.'

18. M. G. Ward, "Kleist's *Der zerbrochne Krug* and Romanticism", *Orbis Litterarum*, 35 (1980), 1 - 27.

19. The reality of the action necessarily dictates a rejection of R. Spörri, *Dramatische Rhythmik in Kleists Komödien*, (Zurich, 1954), p. 20: 'So lange die Konvention ungestört war, d.h. Eves Ehre nicht geschändet, stand der Krug unversehrt auf seinem Platze.'

20. On these grounds D. Grathoff's conclusion appears questionable, "Der Fall des Krugs. Zum geschichtlichen Gehalt von Kleists Lustspiel", *Kleist Jahrbuch*, 1981/82, p. 293: 'Sie hat in der Tat, allerdings nicht in sexueller Hinsicht, ihre Unschuld verloren, indem sie, durch Adams Lügen getäuscht, in einen andern Stand der Erkenntnis geraten ist.'

21. This issue is avoided by K. L. Schneider, "Heinrich von Kleists Lustspiel *Der zerbrochene Krug*" in *Das deutsche Lustspiel*, I, edited by H. Steffen, (Göttingen, 1968), p. 177: 'Der Krug besitzt sicher mancherlei symbolische Bedeutung, doch wird er im Laufe der Handlung immer mehr zum bloßen Anlaß für die verwickelten Vorgänge.'

22. The more significant exceptions to this are H. Arntzen, *Die ernste Komödie. Das deutsche Lustspiel von Lessing bis Kleist*, (München, 1968), pp. 178 - 200, and R. Labhardt, *Metapher und Geschichte. Kleists dramatische Metaphorik bis zur "Penthesilea" als Widerspiegelung seiner geschichtlichen Position*, (Kronberg, 1976), pp. 176 - 98.

23. In particular, a reexamination of the potential symbolic resonance of the pitcher may provide an answer to the problem neatly summarised by E. Wendt, "O Himmel - Zu einigen Wörtern in Kleists 'Zerbrochenem Krug'", *Kleist Jahrbuch*, 1984, p. 63: 'Aber am Ende bleibt der Krug

zerbrochen und der Wunsch, es möchten Sitte, Ehre, Recht, Vertrauen ineins fallen, unerfüllt. Und damit die Frage, ob es denn eine Komödie oder eine Tragödie ist, unbeantwortet.'

24.   Heinrich Gessner, "Der zerbrochne Krug. Idylle nach Salomon Gessner" reproduced in *Heinrich von Kleist, Der zerbrochne Krug*, edited by R. H. Samuel, (London, 1950), pp. 113 - 5.

25.   H. Zschokke, "Der zerbrochene Krug. Eine Erzählung" reproduced in *Heinrich von Kleist, Der zerbrochne Krug*, edited by R. H. Samuel, (London, 1950), pp. 126f.

26.   Ibid., pp. 137f.

27.   Schiller, VII, 7f.

28.   Schiller, VII, 57f.

29.   The *Variant* is to be found in Vol. I, 839 - 55.

30.   This is a complete inversion of Seidlin's position, op. cit., p. 86: 'What we learn of the pitcher's life throughout more than a century is the fact that here was an indestructible Oneness that defied everything.'

31.   Similarly, this conclusion inverts Grathoff's conclusion, op. cit., p. 298: 'Wie Frau Marthe im anschließenden Bericht über die weitere Geschichte des Kruges schildert, hat er in den unwahrscheinlichsten Situationen die Anfechtungen durch äußere Mächte überstanden . . . Bei diesen Ereignissen hätte er, der Logik natürlicher Gesetze zufolge, eigentlich zerbrechen müssen . . .'

32.   *Friedrich Schiller: On the Aesthetic Education of Man*, edited by E. M. Wilkinson and L. A. Willoughby, (Oxford, 1967), pp. 284f.

33.   Schiller, X, 371.

34.   Schneider, op. cit., p. 170, goes to the other extreme from those who privilege the potential tragedy of the material by marginalising it: 'Bei dieser Umkehrung des Themas entstehen nicht etwa nur einzelne lustspielhafte Situationen, sondern es entwickelt sich eine Komödie, in der die ursprünglichen tragischen Konsequenzen nur noch als Möglichkeit vorübergehend oder am Rande sichtbar werden.'

35.   See F. Güttinger, *Die romantische Komödie und das deutsche Lustspiel*, (Frauenfeld/Leipzig, 1939), p. 220, and R. E. Helbling, *The Major Works of Heinrich von Kleist*, (New York, 1975), p. 55: 'The Broken Pitcher is set in the homespun atmosphere of a little Dutch village; its characters are drawn with their personal idiosyncrasies, their fate entangled in the network of their modest daily pursuits.'

36.   Kleist's use of the analytic technique cannot be dismissed as

simply as H. M. Wolff suggests, "Der zerbrochene Krug und König Oidipus", *MLN*, 54 (1939), 272: '*Der Zerbrochene Krug* ist ein gewöhnliches Konfliktsdrama, in dem einige Voraussetzungen aus technischen Gründen in die Vergangenheit zurückverlegt sind.'

37. F. Martini, "Johann Elias Schlegel: Die stumme Schönheit. Spiel und Sprache im Lustspiel. Mit einem Anhang: 'Einige Überlegungen zur Poetik des Lustspiels'" in *Wesen und Formen des Komischen im Drama*, edited by R. Grimm and L. Berghahn, (Darmstadt, 1975), pp. 303 - 65, and "Bauformen des Lustspiels", op. cit.

38. A. M. Reh, "Der komische Konflikt in dem Lustspiel *Der zerbrochne Krug*" in *Kleists Dramen*, edited by W. Hinderer, Stuttgart, 1981), pp. 93 - 113.

39. Martini, "Johann Elias Schlegel", op. cit., p. 339.

40. Cf. E. Hoffmeister, *Täuschung und Wirklichkeit bei Heinrich von Kleist*, (Bonn, 1968), p. 26: 'Diese Komik beruht auf dem Kontrast zwischen dem betrügerischen Schein, den Adam zur Rettung seiner Haut aufrechterhalten muß, und den wahren Verhältnissen der Wirklichkeit.'

41. See Schrimpf, op. cit., p. 349: 'Diese Prozeßform verleiht den die Komik auslösenden Kontrasten, die ihrer Natur nach dazu neigen, sich in einzelne Situationen und Szenen zu verselbstständigen, Einheit und Zusammenhang.'

42. H. Bergson, *Le Rire. Essai sur la signification du comique*, (Paris, 1969), p. 29.

43. See, for example, J. Milfull, "Oedipus and Adam - 'Der zerbrochene Krug'", *GLL*, 27 (1973 - 74), 7 - 17. W. Schafewaldt, "'Der zerbrochene Krug' von Heinrich von Kleist und Sophocles' 'König Ödipus'" in *Heinrich von Kleist*, edited by W. Müller-Seidel, (Darmstadt, 1967), pp. 279 - 295.

44. L. Jekels, "On the Psychology of Comedy" in L. J., *Selected Papers*, (London, 1952), p. 425.

45. M. Grotjahn, *Beyond Laughter*, (New York, 1957), p. 526.

46. It is, then, not just a question of parody as is suggested by M. Schunicht, "Heinrich von Kleist. 'Der zerbrochene Krug'", *ZDP*, 84 (1965), pp. 550f.: '. . . wie sehr Kleist hier eine dramatische Technik parodiert, die der Klassik als kaum wiederholbares Vorbild tragischer Gestaltungsmöglichkeit galt.'

47. See, for example, W. Wittkowski, "'Der zerbrochene Krug': Gaukelspiel der Autorität, oder Kleists Kunst, Autoritätskritik durch Komödie zu verschleiern', *Sprachkunst*, 12 (1981), 115: 'Nur weil er anwesend ist, kommt Adams Fallversuch

zutage.'

48. Cf E. L. Stahl, *Heinrich von Kleist's Dramas*, (Oxford, 1948), p. 73: 'Kleist invented the figure of the commissioner of justice in order to introduce the element of compulsion into the dramatic action of his comedy.', and Schadewaldt, op. cit., p. 319, who equates Walter with the figure of Apollo.

49. See J. M. McGlathery, *Desire's Sway. The Plays and Stories of Heinrich von Kleist*, (Detroit, 1983), p. 52: 'Like older Italian comedies, Kleist's humorous play concludes with young love's triumph over the sexual jealousy of the older generation.'

50. See Schunicht, op. cit., p. 562, who observes the structural point of the correspondence between individual episode and the overall structure of the drama: 'Kleist ersetzt die herkömmlichen Aktbogen durch einzelne Handlungsphasen, von denen jede Grundzüge des Geschehens bündelt.'

51. While it is easy to share Schunicht's opinion, op. cit., p. 551: 'Adam ist von Kleist keinesfalls als Bösewicht gemeint. Zu offensichtlich geht es dem Dichter um die Komik, die seine Hauptgestalt ausstrahlt', it is important to recognise that Adam is also a very threatening and potentially disturbing character.

52. This conclusion stands in direct opposition to that reached by W. Wittkowski, "*Der zerbrochene Krug*: Juggling of Authorities" in *Heinrich von Kleist-Studien*, op. cit., p. 79: '... the suggested purchase of a new jug while the broken one stays broken signals and symbolizes precisely the end result of the "comedy": faith in the authorities is restored ...'

53. Cf the reservations of J. Ellis, *Heinrich von Kleist. Studies in the Character and Meaning of his Writings*, (Chapel Hill, 1979), p. 124: 'The marriage of the two ... is scarcely an unambiguously good conclusion of the play; they do not look as if they belong together, Ruprecht does not seem worthy of Eve, and we are left with the feeling that she deserves much better than this unattractive individual.'

54. See W. M. Merchant, *Comedy*, (London, 1972), p. 53: 'There is clearly a related rhythm between the annual pattern of pagan and Christian rite: equally clearly comedy echoes this mythic pattern.'

55. Cf. F. Gundolf, *Heinrich von Kleist*, (Berlin, 1922), p. 63: 'Im Zerbrochenen Krug waltet eine kriminelle Einzelspannung in einem besonderen Milieu - beide ohne Horizont, nur getragen von der technischen Meisterschaft.'